Ann Redfearn is a writer, acupuncture practitioner and spiritual healer. Always with an eye on the esoteric, Ann has a deep passion for spiritual knowledge, and has studied many forms of healing and spirituality. She taught Tai Chi for a number of years before following in the footsteps of her beloved father to become an acupuncturist. This subject held a deep fascination as she began her studies at the College of Traditional Acupuncture. She discovered a hidden world of ancient wisdom which has underpinned her practical knowledge and proved to be of profound help in the care and treatment of patients.

To all seekers of truth.

As I review my life, I do so with an ever-growing awareness that I could not have done it alone. I could not have walked this path without you beside me, without your guidance, your love, your challenges, your urges for growth. And so I ask, and ask again – 'Who are You'?

My life has been, and is, an ever-deepening journey of Soul, a testimony to the Spirit of something much greater than I. It is to this Spirit, to that whom I have come to know as God, that I dedicate my life, and my unfolding journey.

With this in mind, this book will be, to a large extent, autobiographical, but is prompted by an urge to share something, and thus to return something of the blessings which have been given to me. It is through our stories that we learn about one another. It is the stories of life that give texture and meaning to my work as a healer and acupuncturist, and my relationships as mother, wife, friend, sister, daughter. I am daily humbled, fascinated, entranced and moved by each person's story of their own life. Each is very 'real' and each is personal and emotional. We live a paradox of being both unique, and of sharing the same stories.

We are emotional beings, experiencing pain, joy, and all that comes in between, and it is these very emotions that unite us all, the world over. As I experience joy, I feel yours; as I experience heartbreak and trauma, I am broken enough to feel yours.

Ann Redfearn

RIVERS OF LIGHT

JOURNEY OF SOUL THROUGH THE WISDOM OF THE FIVE ELEMENTS

AUSTIN MACAULEY PUBLISHERS™

LONDON * CAMBRIDGE * NEW YORK * SHARJAH

A CIP catalogue record for this title is available from the British Library.

ISBN 9781528958417 (Paperback)
ISBN 9781398403413 (ePub e-book)

www.austinmacauley.com

First Published 2022
Austin Macauley Publishers Ltd®
1 Canada Square
Canary Wharf
London
E14 5AA

My thanks go to the kind and dedicated teachers of Five Elements at the College of Traditional Acupuncture in Warwickshire. You opened my senses and my heart and challenged me beyond measure to learn and integrate the language of the Five Elements into my practice and into my life. My thanks too to all of my loved ones and friends and to the many patients and seekers who continue to come my way. I walk with you for a while, and you all share something of yourselves, helping me to piece together the great puzzle of life.

Thank you to my daughter, Emily. You have patiently read my manuscript, helping to shape it and bring it to life. You are encouraging and infinitely kind.

Thank you to Claire Cotterill for the swan logo.

My thanks and gratitude go to the team at Austin McCauley who have brought my vision into being.

A Testimony to Spirit

Rest, but don't stay…

Rest, you say, but don't stay there.
Don't stay in the wreckage of your damage.
Move through and beyond.
Move and keep moving through to the unknown future.
Leave the tattered past where it belongs.
Please do not martyr yourself to your own pain,
but move as gently as you need to.

Keep moving through and beyond the pain…
Rest, you say, but don't stay there.

Introduction

I've learnt a lot in my 60 short years. I've learnt that I can change how I feel. I've learnt that life is a series of choices, rather than something that is 'done' for us or to us. I've learnt to be awake and conscious, and once awake, I cannot go back, I must continue. I've learnt that life is incredible, maddening, heart breaking, ecstatic. But most of all, I've learnt that life is a big mirror. It is a mirror on such a huge scale that until we realise it's there, we don't even see it. This mirror of miracles reflects what we need to see. It shows us again, again and yet again who we are. It reveals our deepest darkest, most hidden shadows. It reveals the energetic continuum that we and our life events and close relationships have created.

The Oracle at Delphi famously states 'Know Thyself,' a theme built on by Socrates who tells us that, 'The unexamined life is not worth living.' The greatest task is to find routes and paths, mirrors and reflections that can fulfil this challenge. Only we can change our own unique shape, but to honour the journey of Soul, this shape must first be understood.

What follows is a bit of a tale. It's a tale of one life, so tiny, such a fragment, the tiniest grain of sand in the massive beach of time. Yet that life is mine, and it's all I truly have. As with all of us, the people around me who fill my heart with love are borrowed and they are borrowed so that I can truly learn how to love.

It's also a tale of 'shapeshifting', and although the idea sounds simple, the task of changing our shape can prove to be a path beset by the challenge of personal discovery and far from easy. The shape we have created determines both how life and the people within it, who are very close to our hearts, will react, respond and ultimately treat us. Of course, we may often rant, rage and expound on the unfairness of our life, or how terribly this person with their bad attitudes and behaviour has treated us, our clanging mind and turbulent emotional self seeks to deny our part in any of this. They determinedly defend our position, justifying why we are so right and others, those terrible perpetrators of hurt, are wrong. "It's not my fault!" the emotions cry. "It's them!" shouts the disorientated mind.

This way can prove tumultuous and exhausting. It can be diminishing and distracting. It's distracting because it takes attention away from what life is really all about. Beneath the often wounded and deeply hurt 'show', there is something else. Something miraculously enduring. Something with such patience, such grace, such benevolence; something that catches us when we fall and wraps us in its arms.

This 'something' is love. As children, we seek love from parents, as growing adults, from lovers and spouses. As we grow further, we seek it from our own children, from friends and co-workers. If we have learnt anything along the way, we have also learnt how to give the love that we seek. As life rattles us, challenges and occasionally assaults us, then we often turn to a different kind of love.

"God, why did you let this happen to me?" we plead. We begin prayers of beseeching, begging for happiness and everything else that we crave, seeking out this force of goodness that we've heard so much about, begging God to sort it all out, and do it all for us. After all isn't it our birthright to be happy and loved? Well-meaning friends tell us that we 'deserve' it, so what's going wrong?

I had thought that I was a pretty good kind of person. My quiet times and personal life had been dedicated to spiritual questing and deep inner searching since a very early age. As a child, I was fascinated by faith healers, fairies and nature. My whole life has had spiritual growth as its backdrop. I was a Sunday school teacher when my own children were little, as attending church was a staple in my life. I expanded my thinking through books on Buddhist teachings, books on healing and energy work – you name it, I explored it and integrated it into my life. I studied and taught Tai Chi and worked as a massage therapist, but always endeavoured to put the needs of my family first. I studied for seven years under a Tibetan Meditation teacher and shaman.

I went on to study acupuncture and expanded on this profound training by gaining a qualification in Esoteric Healing. I was always ready to 'jump' at the call of need, particularly from my family and close friends. I loved my children with such a passion, that nothing was too much trouble. My love for my children pulled me through many times of darkness. All in all, I thought I had done 'enough' to understand what it was all about. Yet, despite all the healings, the 'inner work' and my best efforts, the deep meditations and release of demons, and many other wonderful techniques, my 'patterns' of distress (you could call them karma) kept rising again and again, often on more subtle levels. Heavily disguised, they would seep under my door. 'Here I am again! I don't believe it.' I would cry in desperation, 'I thought I'd got to the bottom of all that.' I'm sure many of you know this frustration all too well. It's one that scores of us on the path of awakening share.

There are many and varied teachers and teachings along this path, and one of these teachers is the perseverance required to keep on going. Despite setbacks, pitfalls, depression and despondency, a mysterious something urges us on. I call this teacher, Dedication, and as I shall describe later in the book, this is a quality of the spirit of earth – a deep commitment to the self as an individual.

The humbling news is that I now feel as though I really am breaking free of my patterns and reshaping myself on a deeper and more lasting level. As I look back at the person I was, I'm much nicer now! The Tibetan meditation teacher used to say to us, "Just be kind. Anyone who is truly kind doesn't need all this spiritual stuff. If you can't be truly kind, then be selfishly kind, in other words, know that you will receive merit for good works and kind deeds, and that you will ultimately benefit." There were three of us in this exclusive little group, and I could feel us all thinking the same, *Well, I'm truly kind! Can't he see it? Surely, he doesn't mean me?* Hmm, there was a way to go for all of us, but we're all getting somewhere with that now.

Kindness must extend to the self. Everything begins and ends with the individual, you or me, so here is where the pathway of love begins. Here with your beautiful self. Here with your hurts, your aches and your pains. Here, with the multiple layers of distress and disappointments, dreams broken, heart shattered. Here is where the healing truly begins. Love will take you as you are. Love will accept everything about you. No need to hide any longer. Love will blossom and flourish through you and around you, healing and restructuring and making you whole again. Love will freshen your skin and bring a sparkle to tired eyes. It will reignite your life, giving colour to the drabbest of days. It will change you from the inside out.

Perhaps, the most healing gift of love is unconditional acceptance. If I truly love you, I will accept you in your entirety, with your beauty, your pain and your struggles. I will not judge you but will strive to support and sustain your thriving and your growth. I will celebrate your triumphs with unbridled joy and hold you up when you fall. And if you truly love me, then you will give me the same. Can you do this for yourself? Can you love and accept yourself unconditionally? Can your love emerge from your heart as a gentle but steady flame through all life's blessings and pitfalls?

I am learning this gracious art. It takes skill and practice and sometimes I stumble and fall and must pick myself up again and carry on. I'm getting the hang of it now and feel so very much better in every area of my life. When I am centred in my heart, the world takes on a different resonance. It becomes more fluid, more colourful, certainly easier and very much more peaceful. Old feelings of angst, agitation, frustration and irritation melt away. It is as though I step into a different realm. Perhaps this is what really does happen. The resonance of love is on a high frequency and will take you away from the heavy mundane world. It will lift you to a different energetic reality. This is the realm of healing, miracles and manifestations of your higher dreams.

How do we get there? For me, love came on the wings of a deepening in my understanding of who I am and what makes me tick. This understanding has called a halt to the endless critical mind games of judging myself, blaming myself and forever finding myself wanting. It has put an end to the addictive striving to be 'better' and has brought me to a place of inner peace, and although I may stray from here from time to time, and sometimes for longer than others, it is now an intrinsic part of my makeup and easy to return to. I have had many 'Aha' moments. "So this is why I feel/think/behave... like I do."

When I answered a deep calling of my soul to study acupuncture, I was introduced to a hidden and magical world. This world has its own language and tools of discovery. Its language is of the Five Elements, and I was taken down an extraordinary path. At first, this seemed complex to my untrained senses, but now seems as natural as life itself, and indeed, to this way of being is life itself. I would like to simplify the theoretical side and show you how each of the Five Elements arises in life and in you, blending and weaving to create the beautiful incredible individual that is you. My deepest hope is that this way of knowing will bring you to the same point that it has brought me to, a place of profound acceptance.

The way of the Five Elements informs my acupuncture treatments, as now the person in front of me, far from being a set of symptoms and pain, becomes the embodiment of the gifts and challenges of life. We arise from nature and these forces of nature (called different phases of qi in acupuncture terminology) live in and around us in a constant state of flux, having a direct effect not only on our health and wellbeing, but on the personal lens, or perspective, through which we each live our lives. Each person, although an infusion of all the five elements has a natural affinity with one of the elements, and this element can act as a mentor along the road of personal discovery.

Those of us on this path of self-discovery and awakening probably feel both blessed and at times severely challenged as we stumble this way and that. We live in a time when the doorways to what was once hidden or sacred knowledge have creaked open and we can choose from a huge array of ancient and modern philosophy, religion and self-help techniques. The glory of this is that many of us are rather an eclectic mix of East meets West, Ancient and New Age. The down side is that so many 'tools' have come out of the closet, that we are liable to become confused as we flounder from one to another. The pathway of the five elements does not distinguish between East or West or tells us that one pathway or religious view is better or worse than another. Five Elements is a pathway of the story of humanity, with its many and varied gifts, challenges, blessings and difficulties. It underpins all our life stories, allowing for all our differences, whilst bringing us all together into the richness of what it means to be human and alive. It can prove to be a path of deepening awareness of you as an individual, showing the way to resolve and make peace with the deeper aspects that are sometimes referred to as karma.

I have trodden many paths in my search for knowledge and truth, all of which have enriched my life in some way, but the path of the Five Elements offers a 'realness' that I can fully incorporate and has become my way of choice. I can live with it in my everyday existence, not having to confine it to special times because it lives and breathes in the world around me as well as within my own being. I can also integrate it well into my personal spirituality and my own relationship with the divine. The theory is not based on religion but is rooted deeply in the natural world from which we have emerged and which day by day, hour by hour, minute by minute, supports our lives. From my own perspective, it enhances, rather than diminishes my spiritual practices, adding a wonderful depth and a breadth to my understanding of myself and other people.

Many of us in our frantically paced lives gaze outwards towards nature, almost as a separate event, or something that lives outside ourselves that we may notice in passing. Here, in the world of the five elements we are invited inwards to discover how nature lives not only around, but within each of us, uniting us all with all other aspects of life. For those of us who are spiritual or religious, God is natural law, and the wonder of the creative forces. The divine is you and is me and lives within and without in this ceaseless spiral of beauty and creation.

An integral part of the dance of life is the opportunity that it presents to understand and to know ourselves as we begin to see teachings and processes reflected back from nature and mirrored within ourselves. It can be through these mirrors that life reflects what many have come to know as karma. Life patterns itself around the shapes that we create and as we keep recreating the same experience, we began to see patterns of karma arising, and with this knowledge, comes the potential to release and to heal old and restrictive patterns.

Living as we do in this urbanised and rapidly changing world, the call to return to nature for answers is perhaps just what we need in order to find our internal rhythm and a way of balancing the huge pressures that life in this modern age daily throws in our direction. We find ourselves just about as far removed from nature as we can be. We live in artificially heated and air-conditioned environments, surviving on fast food, as we dash on public transport or in cars through heavily polluted environments. The world is now 24/7 and the endless hubbub becomes relentless as we move seamlessly from computer screen to TV to mobile phone, games consoles etc. etc. It goes on and on. Every now and again something inside tells us to press the pause button, take stock, reset, realign and look for what is missing in our lives.

The way of the Five Elements is the way of balance. We are called upon in a profound way, to find a point of balance and to stay there regardless of what life on the outside throws at us. We live in deeply transformative times, when the turbulence of the world seems threatening and overwhelming. If enough of us answer the call to balance through a strong and loving heart, then the world will to begin to respond. It is the responsibility of each of us to come home now, away from the unsustainability of extremes, towards an approach to our own lives that we can live with.

When I'm working with my patients, a question I ask myself is "What does this person need?" Is it stillness or movement? Is it nurturing or strengthening? The list goes on. I offer you this question to put to yourself. "What do I need to keep my balance?" The call is to know yourself on a deep level so that you no longer trip yourself up but take the path of balanced choice, listening to and observing your responses and reactions. From this point of balance, you can live through your authentic deeper soul self, uncovering gifts that you possibly have only dreamt of.

In my work as a Soul Healing practitioner, I use my knowledge of the five elements to deepen my understanding of the workings and symbology of the Chakra system. Here is where I integrate the Meridian system of acupuncture and the Chakra system of Soul Healing as taught to me. This enables a more holographic picture of a person's energetic matrix to become revealed and for wounds to appear for resolution and perhaps healing. As this happens and obstacles that were previously hidden from view fall away, the soul becomes more able to play a greater role in this person's life, and things can really start to change for the better.

My husband and I were recently on a trip to Barcelona, and he pointed out people taking 'selfies'. They would pull a 'selfie smile' as he named it, sucking cheeks in and looking fabulous and smiley. As soon as the snap was taken, they would change and become a sagging, miserable everyday kind of self. It was so marked. I wonder what we are doing to ourselves as we continually split from the everyday self into a 'selfie' self that we deem acceptable to the outside world. It seems at best deeply unhealthy and at worst a tragedy. We are told that the growing epidemic is of mental and emotional health crises, which seems almost inevitable if we continue in this vein of pressure, 'unrealness' and internal division. It takes a certain courage to begin to reconnect, but the rewards are well worth the effort and dedication needed to take this journey. Courage is needed to cut through the invisible cords of emotion that tell us that we need to be other than who we truly are.

How to become authentic? The secret lies in three simple words: compassion, balance, harmony. When all these three are flowing through all aspects of you, life becomes purified of dense and dark difficulties, and the authentic you can at last spread its wings and begin to emerge. Life begins to transform into a never-ending spiral of change and beauty. Things take on a different flavour as now you can begin to become witness to, and a participant in, the glorious dance of life.

I invite you to take a little time to come with me on this journey of discovery, or should I say 're-discovery', because there is a deep part of every person that already understands the laws of the natural world. It is perhaps that deeply hidden and forgotten part that longs to run in the hills, swim in the oceans, jump through puddles or stop to gasp over a glorious sunset. It is that part which is perhaps reserved for 'leisure', for weekends and holidays. The pathway of Five Elements can help to soften these boundaries, showing how nature communicates every day through each one of us.

My desire is to present the Five Elements to you in a way that transports it from a classical theory, being used in a few select acupuncture clinics, to a fantastically rich story of life that you can integrate easily into your own values, religions and personal growth. It is a journey of life and therefore richly healing and rewarding. I wish you happy travelling and hope that you enjoy this incredible and magical experience of living as much as I do.

Using This Book

This book serves as both an introduction to and an overview of the living energy of the Five Elements as I see and experience them through my own life and the lives of my patients. The chapters on each of the elements begins with a lyrical presentation of the spirit of the element as an aspect of soul. They can each be read separately as introduction to the chapter but can also be pieced together as a meditation to show the progression of the spirit through the seasons of life.

These meditations came to me with such ease, flowing their way through to my keyboard as though writing themselves. They came while I was sitting under our beautiful and enormous willow tree which is growing in the middle of our natural pond. I was surrounded by the elements of life, and they wrote their song through me. The writing of this book spanned all the seasons. I began writing it in winter, the time of the water element. I then progressed through spring, summer, late summer and autumn, feeling and expressing the movements and phases of nature as a dance of life within and around me. I have chosen words, phrases and a change of pace to express, and to invoke, the energy of each element. My hope is that in this way you will be able to feel the changes around and within you and get to know your own resonances even better.

I present each element as spirit or essence and show how they resonate with certain processes of body, mind and emotions. I have described their shadowy, denser sides which both emerge from and are revealed through the challenges and difficulties we all face in the course of our lives. Challenge can be the best of teachers when it comes to finding out about who we truly are, and it's through the lens of acceptance and compassion that we can see our darkest and hidden sides, and ultimately, without shame, bring them to the light. I have gone on to describe what can happen as this heaviness lifts, making way for lighter flows of qi. I have described the different stages of completion, or 'enlightenment' as a path of initiation for the evolving soul as it moves towards its higher consciousness.

On rising out of the difficult and dense arenas of learning, the elements awaken to a more 'heavenly' or rarefied realm, each one manifesting as a virtue and together creating a more 'enlightened' way. To become enlightened is to become whole and healed as you encompass all aspects of self with loving acceptance. Sometimes problems that have caused struggles, including physical symptoms, spontaneously disappear with changes in qi, and sometimes it's our attitudes and outlook that changes, allowing us to deal more effectively with challenges.

It may be helpful to use this book 'seasonally' to understand the movements of qi that live within and around you. It may be that you feel an affinity with one or two of the elements and wish to place your attention there. You may recognise yourself and some of your traits in one or more, or indeed in all of the elements, and I hope that this proves helpful in the process of knowing of yourself. The task of the 'enlightened' is to encompass all the elements in equal balance, creating a platform through which the healed and balanced soul can shine its light out into life. This can be a long path for some and not for others. There is no sense of competition or of making things too 'real', just an opening towards a growing awareness of who you really are.

I hope that it will piece together and unravel some of the questions and the mysteries that you may have about yourself and your own life. The contemplations in this book are designed to take you into the spirit of each element and can be revisited many times as you take your journey. My next aim is to create a more practical presentation of the elements as a handbook that can be used as a companion to this book. The information and ideas that I present to you are, of course, guides to life, and are by no means intended to replace any medical or professional help that you may be receiving, but merely to open up some ideas that might be unfamiliar to you.

Take hold of,
absorb the potent essences of nature through attuning
with the five elements
of the world in which we live.
Look around you at the cycles of beauty, strength and
wisdom as one season reaches towards the next.
Then discover these qualities within yourself…

Where Is Your Wound, Sweet Soul?

Where is your wound, sweet Soul, where is your wound?
Why do you weep, sweet Soul,
Why do you weep?
Where did you break,
Where did you shatter,
Who took from you the things that matter?
Who took your light,
Who took your spark,
Why do you walk alone in your dark?
Who took the joy from out of your hands
and bid you wander in barren lands?
I call you back with a cry from my heart,
To stand in your truth and reclaim your spark.
I call you to remember who you really are,
From the depths of the earth to the light of the stars…
To remember, remember, remember
Who you truly are…

Foreword

Dean Clarke

Orange St Practice

Uppingham

Like a sparkling fairy, landing in the centre of a magical daisy circle she arrived, and Annie and I joined energies whilst training together in the Warwickshire countryside at The College of Traditional Acupuncture. Her innocent radiance beamed brightly as we discovered the joys and healing transformation of the Five Elements.

The founder of the College of Traditional Acupuncture, CTA, as it came to be known, was Professor J R Worsley. He pioneered Five Elements Acupuncture practice in the UK, collating detailed information from his overseas travels, to support his theory that we all live in a close relationship to the seasonal and elemental changes revealed in nature. He put forward the proposition that we are all a blend of the Five Elements of nature, but that just one element in particular reveals itself as being predominant. When a person is treated through that element, it puts everything back in order encouraging a balance in body, mind and spirit. He saw the profound relationship between the seasons, the functional organs within the body and the emotions. He saw how strong feelings such as anger, fear or worry can manifest, creating an imbalance within.

Little did Annie and I then know that this new world of discovery would transform many lives young and old. We continued working together creating a successful Acupuncture Clinic in Birmingham for five years, spreading the Five Element concept through workshops and group talks. We found working together was extremely productive as we could treat many aspects of an individual with a combined energy. Often acupuncture treatments may seem very one dimensional but we seemed to add a more three-dimensional aspect, which meant being able to treat the person from many aspects of being.

Sometimes, for example, Annie would work on the person's emotional state, whilst I would concentrate more on their physical strengths and weakness as well as past and current trauma. Many clients felt the benefits and appreciated the strength it gave, acting like an invisible scaffolding to support and gently move a person forward in their life.

We treated many people; all were welcome through our doors. We encountered varying issues in our day's work, treating anyone and everyone, from young offenders to teachers and professors, with many conditions for us to address, including, autism, cancer, eating disorders, immune system conditions, pain and anxiety but probably the most common thread was people feeling unhappy and frustrated; feeling stuck and not feeling at ease in their own skin.

I think during these years we both realised the importance of balance and respect that is given by both parties, both patient and practitioner, which helps to create amazing changes in body, mind and spirit. We certainly were part of a change in many lives and on many levels.

Part of our work as acupuncture practitioners is to discover the missing link or time when a block in the system may have been created, take the person back to that time, almost like a regression to the point of change, then build them back up to the present day. These blocks can happen at any time, often coming about through strong emotions, and have the effect of restricting the natural flows of energy that connect us and move us through life.

As a Five Elements practitioner, it always fascinates me how many old-fashioned sayings and quotes seem to directly relate to acupuncture theory, as signposts towards where imbalances may lie within our energetic system. Everyday phrases, such as 'Wearing your heart on your sleeve', 'I just can't stomach it anymore!', 'I'm suffocating', 'It knocked the breath right out of me,' or perhaps 'I'm beside myself with rage', can all indicate specific areas of distress within the mind, body or spirit, making a signpost towards where healing needs to take place.

Many of the teaching comes from ancient scripts and drawings that have been translated over the years, making it difficult to have a true and pure translation of the essence of how the workings both physically and mentally were to be understood. However, having worked with these teachings for a number of years, my belief, which is a belief shared by Annie, is that the essence of true wisdom and healing comes from within.

A frequently used acupuncture point within our practices is called Stomach 36 – Zu San Li, which translates as Leg Three Miles. Treating this point is said to give the patient the stamina and capacity to keep going those extra three miles in life. It is understood this point was used on great expeditions to give a boost of energy when the legs were getting tired – hence Leg three Miles – giving longitude to the tiredness.

I find in our modern world, music can also be related to areas that may need attention in a person's life. I often see joggers with earphones listening as they run. If we carefully listen to our favourite tracks, we will find hidden messages of love, hurt, strength, betrayal etc. Modern technology allows us to group these together in playlists. Wouldn't it be wonderful to have our seasonal change supported by a playlist to move us gracefully and tunefully from spring though to winter, however, the chances are, that you have already instinctively created it, as your tastes change to reflect the changes in nature. Often the greatest hits are put straight to the top because so many people can personally relate to them *'Love is All Around'* was a huge international success, spending 15 weeks at the top of the British charts.

With an increase in interest in mindfulness and meditation, we are beginning to tune in to our inner thoughts and strengths to discover an intuitive way forward. These subconscious depths are very much part of us – "When a child is born into this life, it has no concept of the tone of skin its living in," says the well-known song. We learn emotional responses, such as fear, anger, worry. These emotions arise from within and are nurtured into reality by life events. As we grow older, we learn to adapt and change but fundamentally the early life teachings provide the foundations. These sometimes needs to be re-framed in order to create balance at a deeper level.

We take it for granted that our body will work in total synchronicity, and that unless something major happens, it will correct itself without intervention. The link between body, mind and soul is built delicately and carefully over a period of time in which we discover our likes and dislikes through carefully selected choices. Nature provides us with unlimited offerings of seasons to live by and it makes complete sense to me for us all to re connect with nature in order to awaken the person within.

Annie's teachings are heartfelt with warmth and compassion that will enlighten the reader with her sensitivity and deep emotional values. Her gentle, mystical approach ensures that we have a safe space in which to explore contemplation and mind-provoking thoughts leaving us inspired and truly comforted.

I wish my esoteric sister well with yet another fascinating insight into a new world of bright and empowering words.

Words of heartfelt love and more importantly, words to live by.

Thank you JR!

(Professor J.R. Worsley)

While studying Five Elements Acupuncture at the College of Traditional Medicine near Warwick in England, I and my fellow students soon had impressed upon us the significance of Professor J.R. Worsley (affectionately known as JR), who introduced this style of acupuncture practice to the UK.

The theory of Five Elements formed both the theoretical and the practical structure of this approach to health. Its origins remain something of a mystery, because at the time when JR was studying acupuncture, no official training of this kind was available in the UK. He travelled to Taiwan, Singapore and Korea to explore, research and understand this form of treatment, going on to establish the College of Traditional Acupuncture in the UK in the 1950s. He opened other teaching colleges in the USA and some European countries and also lectured extensively in the UK and abroad to share with contagious enthusiasm the incredible knowledge that he had gained.

The theory of his teaching was founded on the premise that the forces of nature live and breathe within each of us, and when they are in perfect balance, good health can be achieved that is harmonious and flowing with possibilities.

The five elements, Wood, Fire, Earth, Metal and Water are not just the foundation of this wonderful system of medicine: they are the foundation and spirit of all nature around us… The Elements are alive both around us and in us; they describe the movement of all life and all energy and embody all the qualities which we encounter in nature. Through understanding the Five Elements, we may begin to understand both nature and ourselves…

Looking for the spirit of the Elements in nature is as much about what we can become as about what we are.

The Five Elements and the Officials, J.R. Worsley, p. i and v, 1998, J.R. and J.B. Worsley.

I think I can speak for many other practitioners of Five Elements Acupuncture, when I say that we are greatly indebted to JR and all teachers and tutors of this healing art, notably at the College of Traditional Acupuncture. From my own perspective, this way of understanding the life and health of people, has helped me on a personal level, opening my heart, my mind and my senses to the world of nature. It has been and continues to be the most profound way of living a life of balance and wellbeing.

Thank you JR, and thank you to all who have succeeded you and have continued your legacy.

Annie Redfearn

Chapter 1

Light and Qi

Imagine for a moment, that you are formed from rivers and streams of light, weaving, cascading and flowing through mind, body and spirit; sometimes moving, sometimes still and silent as pooling lakes, but merging together and creating the story of you and your life. These rivers and streams make up a system, whose task it is to carry energy and light. Together they create an intricate communication network around the entire surface of the skin, forming channels and pathways for the flows of life force. Ancient Chinese philosophers named this life force as qi (pronounced chee), and through their observations, perceived it as circulating and swirling in beautiful waves through the whole of the natural world qi, like water, needs routes along which to flow, and these pathways within the mind, body and spirit of each of us are known as the meridians.

Understanding Qi

Qi is life power and spirit, and as a living force streams through all beings, weaving and spiralling its dance of life. Just as water courses through and upon the surface of this planet, so qi moves silently through the body, the emotions and the thoughts, linking mind, body and feelings to the experiences that we all encounter as we move through our individual lives. The ultimate expression of qi, and that which many of us strive towards, is the creation of a peaceful and harmonious state of being. This will give rise to a pathway to the higher mind, higher consciousness of soul, and ultimately, a merging with that which we think of as divinity.

Take a long slow inhalation.
Imagine that you are immersed in a beautiful world of light.
You are light, and you are materialised form.
You are unique and patterned by your soul and your purpose.

Qi is the light-force that flows through and around all of us, weaving its gifts of beauty and magic. It is the creative and generative force that keeps life flowing through the natural world and the cyclical movements of the seasons and through each one of us in all the seasons of our own and very individual experiences of life. Few people can see this force, but for many of us, it can be detected through increased awareness and sensitivity and often through feeling. The effects of this natural force are not consigned to the world of the sensitives but are there for all to see and to experience. For the majority of us qi is visible though the cycles of nature and the growth and change that we all see and feel in the world around. Look out of your window, and you can see the vitality of nature in the trees that flank the pavements, the flowers that spring up in the hedgerows, in the laughing child, or in the spring in the steps of people who walk by. Healthy qi is the beautiful spirit of happiness and vitality, and wellbeing on all levels of life. It brings the good things to life: joy, abundance, pleasure, prosperity, generosity of spirit.

Qi can be seen through the immense beauty of the natural world, the rapid growth of vegetation and oxygen-producing trees, in the balance and changes in weather conditions and in the cycles that create just the right environment for life to flourish. We need healthy qi for nourishment, and it comes in the form of health-giving crops and sustaining vital foods. Have you ever noticed that freshly picked foods, such as summer vegetables, almost dance with vitality? If you eat these, then of course you will take this vitality straight into your body. If you go outside on a breezy day and take huge deep breaths, then you are taking the vitality of air deeply within. If you swim in the ocean, you can experience the incredibly healing and refreshing effects of the energy of water. And if you revel in the sunlight on a summer's day, how wonderful you feel as your body opens and relaxes in the light and warmth of the live-giving energy of the sun. These are all phases of qi, and so much part of life that we don't really give them the attention that we could.

Qi is everywhere and fuels the natural world which we are a part of. We arise from nature and, and its cyclical laws and are therefore deeply influenced by, and an intrinsic part of these very flows and changes. Life plays its tune in and around us. We can all enjoy the effects of healthy qi, with its natural vigour and creative vitality, supporting both action and rest, and creating the pathways within each of us towards living a fulfilling and happy life. In our environment, whether home or the workplace, a healthy circulation of qi makes all the difference generating a positive and supportive environment for life to flourish. In animals and other creatures of the waters, earth and air, strong flows of qi ensure the ability to thrive and sustain healthy life as vital participants in the cycles of the natural world.

Qi, like air, loves to circulate unimpeded. It flows in whirls and spirals and is the creative power behind movement and change. If qi is not able to move freely and harmoniously, it can become unbalanced, unhealthy and degenerative. When the flow is impeded, disturbed or misdirected, it slows down and can become subject to being blocked, disrupted and at times, stagnant. Disharmonies of qi can be felt and experienced, often arising in people as symptoms of illness and disease or lack of vitality and progress. This state of imbalance can often flow outwards into life, creating difficulties on a greater scale. It can be perceived as lack of harmony in the home, challenges in friendships and relationships or difficulties in the working life.

It can also work the other way – disharmony in your environment can become mirrored as disharmony in your own energy. It's a two-way flow, with each one of us affecting our immediate, and arguably, broader environment, and in turn, this same environment affecting each of us. In this way, it can be seen that we do not live in isolation, but as a circulating flow of energies. Have you noticed that if you are in the presence of a positive and happy person, then your mood and energy lift in response? Have you also noticed that there are some people who have the opposite effect on you, making you want to rapidly distance yourself from them?

We are all highly attuned and sensitive beings, being receptive and responsive and having an in-built awareness of the different levels and qualities of qi. Our natural defence and response mechanisms enable us to process huge amounts of information through our senses and feelings. As we have already discussed, you may be drawn to some people, situations or places, but feel strongly averse to others. I'm quite sure that you have experienced buildings that feel oppressive, or dark dank places that you want to run from. In these places, for whatever reason, qi is unable to flow with its natural healing light and instead becomes unhealthy and subjected to heavier or stagnant energies. You will have encountered people that you just feel 'uncomfortable' around, or whom you instinctively dislike. You will also have encountered people with whom you feel immediately at ease, as though you've known them all your life, and buildings and places where you feel happy and thriving. When you are considering a new home, it is the feeling and the atmosphere that you will respond to and it is this that will make your decision about whether it is right for you.

It is more than likely that we have all had times in life when nothing seems to work out. One thing goes wrong, perhaps the breakdown of a close relationship, and everything else seems to follow, tumbling down like a pack of cards. As if in response to the first thing that went wrong, everything else follows suit, as this level of qi recreates itself. Nothing seems to work, and everything seems to be endlessly dark, difficult, beset with problems. Hopefully, these phases are temporary, and life gets back on an even keel before too long. These difficulties are part of a natural process of learning about ourselves and learning about how life works out along the trajectory of qi that we are following.

There may also be times in life when you have the 'Midas touch' and everything works out easily and beautifully. Nothing seems to go wrong and creating the life you want is almost effortless. You can't put a foot wrong! You have healthy and loving friendships and relationships, you thrive in your chosen work, and feel on top of the world. However, for many people, life is not as separated out as this and can appear a mix of seemingly random of ups and downs. Things can appear inconsistent, one minute up, and the next down.

Life is bumpy and uncoordinated until you begin to take charge of your own flows of energy and to gain some awareness of what's happening, and perhaps why it is happening and the learning that it offers. If all is well on the inside, then regardless of the challenges that life presents, you will retain a level of consistency and harmony.

The Phases of the Elements

Patterns and phases of qi are eloquently communicated and understood through the changing cycles of the seasons. Each season has its own feeling and resonance. Even with our eyes closed, we know when it's summer, spring, or winter, just by the energy and the feeling around. Much as we exist in relationship with our own self and with each other, so each season exists in relationship to the other seasons to create the full cycle of a year. Each season has its own particular gifts and challenges in the cycle of life and death that are wonderfully expressed through the phases of nature. As will be discovered later in this book, each season also relates to, and resonates with, one of the Five Elements, that brings its own particular spirit to that season.

Ancient Chinese Masters learnt from nature by acute observation and experience and began to deeply understand the phases of growth and decay that flow one into the other to create the cycles of life. They recognised five distinct phases, which they linked to the seasons, thus naming five seasons in all, with late summer, or harvest, being recognised as a separate season that sits between summer and autumn. In this way, the philosophy of the five elements was born. The life cycle of qi begins with the element of water which is revealed through the season of winter. Water holds the mystery and potential of life. Life in its myriad forms emerges from water and is dependent upon water for growth and survival. Water therefore represents the most fundamental aspects of life as we know it to be.

As qi progresses from just the potential of an idea into materialised form, it enters the phase of spring and the element wood. This phase fulfils the blueprint of distinct forms of life, which can be experienced as the growth and the emergence of the individual, whether a human, a tree, an insect or the birth of an idea. Wood tells of activity and vigour and is the impetus behind the creation of the rich variety of life. It is the phase of vision and birth.

Qi then progresses towards full maturity through summer and the element fire. This is the phase of exaltation and fullest and most open presentation of itself. Qi cannot rise any higher and expresses itself joyfully with beauty, colour and display. Life reaches its zenith, through the showy blooms of a flower at its most magnificent, or the peak of human experience – it's the 'this is it' moment, the moment we were all born for!

Before the inevitable descent into autumn, qi has a phase of stability, where it is neither ascending nor descending, but acts as a bridge between these two forces of rising and falling. This is the phase of fulfilment, when life spills out of the earth. It is harvest time, or late summer, lazy and warm, ripe with the fruits and abundance of nature. Qi takes its time, as though in gratitude of all that has come to pass, this phase is about the fertility, prosperity, and full expression of life in this materialised plane.

And then begins the descent of the metal element, where qi draws strongly downwards. It is autumn, and time for taking stock and releasing all that is not of value. As natural energy is scarce, only the good, the pure and the true as a strong and worthy foundation is kept. Qi becomes refined and purified, as times of excess of earlier seasons are long gone, and the phase of cold and survival draws near. All the unrefined and unlearnt falls away and decays as leaves falling from a tree. Here is the phase of death, leading towards rebirth and the continuum of life through the water element of winter. In this sense, water holds both the beginning and the end of the cycle.

The cycle repeats itself again and again, one year flowing into the next and so on into a beautiful pattern of life, each phase creating the next, and flowing out of the one that came before. With each year, there is the potential to experience these phases of qi within yourself, and to grow in the understanding of who you are as an expression of life and as a manifestation of your infinite soul. This can be reflected and mirrored through the movements of qi within and around you. Can you feel the rising of the sap on a spring morning as a wave passing through you? How do you feel walking through the woods on a carpet of orange and golden leaves in the autumn? Do rainy, gloomy days affect your mood, and do you long for balmy summer evenings? All these feelings and experiences act as mirrors of the phases of the elements, and as you begin to know the elements, so you will deepen your knowledge of yourself and how you respond to and act as a conduit for the flows of life.

Take a few quiet moments in nature.
Close your eyes for a moment or two
And try to feel the
world around you.
Just by feeling, can you tell which season you are in?
Is the natural energy rising or falling?
What thoughts and feelings does this
phase of qi invoke in you?

We can become familiar with each of the five elements in its own right and gain an understanding of how each of them feels within and around us. We can become familiar with the phases in the cycle of the year that the elements come to express. Each one flows into the next, existing in a very particular relationship with the others, and together ensuring a continuum of harmony, control and balance. As one flows into another, the next season is born, and so on through the cycles of the years. This cycle endures. We can rely on the joy of spring following a harsh and cold winter and can feel the power of sap rising as hope of new things to come. How this is revealed within each of us and the course of our life is explored in depth the course of this book.

The Opposites Polarities of Yin and Yang

This cycle of qi holds and supports the world of nature and is also subjected to the additional forces of yin and yang. As life flows through and between the opposite forces of day and night, so the elements emerge through the opposite forces of yin and yang. Being opposing in nature, they each exert a pull upon the other, and this pull creates movement. It is through this movement that the phases of the elements emerge.

Like the elements, yin and yang exist in their own right, and also in relationship to one another, and like two halves of a puzzle, together they create a whole, which is life. In the context of the elements, the yin phases are the cold and dark times of year and the yang phases are the bright and hot times. Yin has been named as the feminine principle in relation to yang, which is the masculine. Yin is cool, mysterious, slow, dark, quiet and withdrawing, relative to yang, which is rapid, noisy, energised, bright and expansive. Each of the five elements has a predominantly yin or yang movement which serves to direct the flows of qi and create the seasons. The light force of qi is neutral and becomes imprinted by the polarities of yin and yang.

Both polarities of yin and yang are needed for the continuum of life and growth, and both exist in harmony with the other, each moving towards the other as a cycle of flow. Yin moves towards yang, and yang towards yin. Although they appear to be opposites, they each rely on the other and could not exist alone. Imagine the night-time of yin with no daytime of yang to follow? Yin and yang flow one into the other as darkness flows into light, and light into darkness, together creating a balanced whole.

33

As with the qi of the elements, the qi of yin and yang flows throughout life and throughout people. Ancient Masters noted that, regardless of gender, some people were predominantly yin, and others predominantly yang. They observed how the flows of qi correlated with emotional, mental, physical and spiritual characteristics and attributes. They learnt how the qi of each element lives and works through the major organs and processes in the body, becoming revealed through personality traits, emotional tendencies and constitutional strengths and weaknesses. Becoming familiar with yourself as a flow of energies and elements can provide you with a deepening awareness of why you might react as you do, why you make the choices that you do.

What is your particular expression of qi in your life?
Are you a summer or a winter person –
A night owl or a day bird?

The Meridian System

Qi flows through the meridian system in the body, echoing the phases of all the elements which, in turn, echo the phases of the seasons. There are twelve major meridians, which are grouped as pairs. One meridian of the pair is generally yin and one is yang in its movements of qi. Each pairing has a special relationship with an element and through this, with a season. Think of the people in your life who are summery and bright, or who perhaps have a storm cloud lurking over their heads? We often instinctively 'know' the forces of nature that live through people by observing them and by listening to our own feelings in their presence. Think of close friends and family members and try to imagine which season they relate to?

Each season resonates with particular energetic flows and stimulates different meridians, and through these, different aspects of a person emerge on a physical, mental, emotional and spiritual level. For example, the season of summer is the element fire, and this is when summery people feel 'in their element'! They come to life. The fire of summertime is all about love and passion and enthusiasm for life in all its colours. Fire is all about relationships, both friendships and lovers. Fire also governs the heart and circulatory system, and the element of fire can be treated and accessed through the meridian system of fire, which corresponds with the heart and circulatory system.

Elemental Archetype

Each of us is an individual expression of the dance of the elements and, while having an affinity with all, will often have a very particular and special relationship with just one element as a quality of qi. This one element stands out as being a personal archetype, overseeing the pathway of an individual life and providing a lens and a filter of attitudes, beliefs and emotional responses. This archetype runs through all aspects of mind, body and emotions, forging the experiences of life, and giving rise to particular attitudes, challenges and beliefs and creating opportunities for growth, expansion and healing.

A question often posed is whether this archetypal element is with a person all their life, or can it change with personal growth and development? My own view is that it doesn't change and that it exists for the duration of a lifetime. As an archetype, it creates a profound pathway which directs and oversees how life is experienced in an individual incarnation. This is not to say that the experience gained is in any way limited, but it has a definite flavour. This is all governed by the needs of the soul to fulfil certain experiences, and through these to achieve a level of healing and balance. My belief, gained through working with many patients, and though a deepening awareness of my own journey, is that the elemental archetype is the perfect pathway through which the learning through personal karma is experienced.

Karma

Karma is the coming together of light and dark, good and bad, positive and negative and encompasses all of these polarities within each of us is. It is not a judgement but is a great teacher and the means through which balance can be achieved. Karma is the great mirror that says –

> 'All that is received has already been given,
> And all that has been given will also be received.'

By using the metaphor of a mirror or of the reflective nature of water, we can see over time, what in our lives is out of balance and disharmonious, and in this context, what needs attention or healing. Perhaps something that keeps happening to us is also reflected in what we keep doing? It's the same energy, the same level of qi being experienced by what we give and what we receive. The law of karma urges us to look deeply within, rather than to look outside ourselves, but the clues are given though the outside about what needs changing and balancing on the inside. This is a law of resonance. Life is very generous in its efforts to show you, what us, what we need to see.

When an experience repeats itself again and again in a person's life, it is an indication that the soul, or higher self, is trying to understand, express or heal an aspect of itself. This can be thought of as karmic, as the frequent repetition of a state of being indicates that this level is trying to draw attention to itself. Karmic experiences can bring great blessings as well as difficulties.

By looking deeply within, we begin to perceive the karmic threads that run through our lives and, if they bring difficulties, can begin to bring about the changes necessary to heal them. Even just acknowledging that change is needed is sometimes enough to begin the process and is likely to lead you in just the direction that you need. Now, everything that needs to be healed has the potential to be healed, and everything that needs to be forgiven and released is also held in the reflections of life and can be acted upon when circumstances permit, or when the time is right. As healing takes place and the blocks and blind spots of our own limitations fall away, the changes can feel miraculous as higher fields of consciousness become available and life takes on a new and sometimes very different flavour.

Karmic difficulties arise from the hurts and wounds that are gathered throughout incarnations, both present and past. Some of these wounds are so deep that the soul creates a continuum of this wounding, thereby drawing attention to itself as a cry for help. Many of the wounds come in through the deepest and most intimate relationships. It is the people you love the most that can break through to the innermost parts of you, the soft, the trusting and the vulnerable parts. Endings of relationships, violence, abuse and loss of people you love can create deep wounding and despair.

Healing Wounds

Sometimes you may notice the same pattern of hurt emerging again and again throughout your life. "Oh, here I go again," you cry. Many people think of these times as being something negative or 'bad' that needs to be stopped or cut away. They berate themselves for their so-called negative thoughts and behaviours and weaknesses. I take a softer path, understanding that the patterns and shapes that have been created come about through the distortions and discolourations of hurt. How can you beat yourself up for being hurt? Your soul calls out to you to notice the cries of distress and calls you to take steps needed to bring about some healing and balance.

As a pattern rises to conscious awareness, the possibility of addressing and healing it also arises. When authentic healing takes place, it works like magic, repairing damage through all levels of being. Old and disused patterns fall away, there is no longer a need to experience them again, and qi can now flow through the old wounds, creating renewed pathways of light and enabling life to take on a happier, brighter and more prosperous resonance.

The pathway of the spirit of healing is one of authenticity, of reconciling and repairing old wounds and of rising to the highest frequency of your soul path. The call is to become authentic and to accept yourself and others fully and with deep compassion. To be authentic can mean being open and vulnerable as well as being strong and confident. We are all a multi-coloured and multi-textured flow of energy and emotion. Being soft, vulnerable and open can be difficult at times, potentially leaving us unprotected.

We become inauthentic through the need to defend and protect, and very often, only the people we love the most can break through the fortresses that we build around ourselves and our lives. They are built brick by brick as protection from the winter storms of hurt, betrayal, deceit. They are built because of the hurt that has already been experienced, and not wanting any more, you may bunker yourself in and sit tight. You may develop a mask to wear in the outer world, because you are afraid that if you are seen for who you truly are, the world will not like or accept you. How sad. You close down emotionally. You close your heart, focussing on being 'busy' or distracted and, piece by piece, begins the disconnection from who you really are.

You disconnect from the pathway of the soul, from your higher self, from God, Goddess, from the beautiful streams of light that are the birth right of everyone. You may start to become isolated, feeling that no one understands you, and the world seems to pit itself against you. You feel dissatisfied, unfulfilled, lost, exhausted. Life loses its spark, is devoid of meaning, becomes mundane. Depression may set in, as energy become stuck, stale, locked away. You deprive life of your light and live in the world of shadows. You deprive yourself of the potential to be loved, valued, exalted, and for the world to know who you really are. You may hide in mists and clouds, not wanting to be seen.

However, by embracing the mists and shadows of who you are and accepting yourself fully and unconditionally, you give yourself the greatest possible gift.

You begin to move as a whole person and no longer the separated and fractured bits of a person. Become yourself and become whole and allow pathways of qi to flow more wholly and more fully through you and out into your life.

Internal Landscape

Just as different phases of qi are revealed in nature through different climates and weather conditions, so this can be found within each of us. I have come to see the internal world of thought, feeling and emotion as a personal landscape. With its own seasons and climate. Where you choose to live, and the landscapes and environments where you feel most at ease can mirror your internal state and can be a way of understanding yourself more fully.

I live with my husband in a place of water. Water runs down the hill behind our house, cascading through part of the garden as a mini torrent in winter. The house is situated on the banks of a large river. We also have a huge natural pond, and there is a lake just to the side of the garden. Not only this, but for our first two years here the whole garden was deeply flooded as the rivers burst its banks and became part of the generally watery world. I mentioned this to a healer friend, who commented 'Water – so much emotion…!' At the time, this was undeniably true! I have learnt so much from living in such close proximity to water and observing its changeable reflective nature. There is always something happening, nothing stays the same from moment to moment. So refreshing, so alive.

When treating my patients, I tread carefully, taking time to discover who they are inside, beyond their symptoms, seeking to understand the nature and climate of their inner landscape. I try to imagine the weather conditions and whether it is a cityscape or a place in nature. Is it dark or light? Is it cold? Is it damp, warm or sunny? Does it feel welcoming and happy? What's happening there? I sometimes ask my patients to describe their inner world to me. Everyone I ask is very willing, and generally people like to engage in this level of internal discovery. Many people have a love of certain weather conditions, giving vital information about their emotional temperature and it all adds up to helping me to discover how best to approach their treatments.

They may talk to me of beautiful summer rain or crisp white snow on a fresh winter morning. They may love the pulsating intensity of heat and dazzling sunlight, or the dancing of moonlight on gentle seas. Some people like springtime with its promise of something fresh and exciting. Others love beautiful autumn colours that lend grace to the senses before disappearing into the starkness of winter landscapes. Sometimes patients will tell me of a dark or frightening place, perhaps a place they visit in their dreams, and they may become visibly shaken. As they describe the landscape and the weather conditions, I always ask how it feels, as feelings are a vital clue to discovering the person I am with and uncovering their emotional wounds.

Close your eyes,
Giving yourself time to sink deeply within.
Take three deep breaths allowing your internal
landscape to appear before you.
Allow your senses to awaken to take in sounds,
textures, aromas, feelings.
Stay there until you understand.
Stay until you know every detail
Permit yourself to make any changes,
as you freely create a haven of profound
beauty that is yours to experience.
A place of safety.
An inner sanctuary.
A place to return to.

In addition to addressing physical symptoms and conditions, I find that treatments are more successful, and generally longer lasting, when a connection has been made with a patient on a deeper level. I seek to connect with my patients' spirit by interpreting the language of qi that speaks on the more subtle levels. Qi communicates through the senses and reveals itself in and throughout a person in many ways. Training to become a practitioner of traditional acupuncture requires that we train our senses as well as our brains, which is

39

perhaps the most difficult part of the training. It was difficult to reawaken those natural senses which, for many of us, had closed down for any number of reasons. This realisation in itself was profound for me as I began to appreciate people and life through different lenses and not through just my mind.

The rich language of the qi of a person's archetypal element can show itself in many ways as it strives to communicate in ways in which it can become understood. Distress can become revealed through repetitive symptoms, such as pain and discomfort, as it strives to draw attention to itself. The language also extends towards other aspects, and perhaps the most revealing is the emotional world of the patient. The emotions determine how life is approached and is arguably the platform through which life is played out. This language of qi speaks through the movements of the body, through the sound of the voice, the tone and colour of the complexion and through the aroma, which may be detected in the air around the person or may be more physical in nature.

Through my training and through learning the language of the language of the elements, I can usually develop an understanding of where the distress or area of imbalance arises from. Where is the lack of harmony, where the disruption or blockage? It follows that if one area in a person is distressed, perhaps for example from a painful injury, then this will put other or all aspects of that person under pressure. Pain with a known cause can prove to be fairly straightforward to treat and, if this is the case, I would choose my acupuncture points accordingly and the symptoms should disappear fairly quickly, depending on its nature, and balance throughout the whole system should become re-established.

Difficulty arises when the pain is more chronic in nature. Unless it has arisen from a previous known cause, then this level of pain can prove to be an indication of emotional distress. This patient will need a different approach, and I would treat my patient on an emotional level, in addition to giving attention to the pain. Occasionally, I come across pain that comes from a different level of being. It arises from the spirit and is persistent, difficult. Nothing can shift it, and no amount of treatment makes more than a superficial difference. With these patients, there is something about them that tells me that they have become 'obsessed', or 'possessed' by their own pain. There is often fear on a deeper level, or emotional obsession or trauma. Hope seems to have gone out of their eyes, and they appear resigned, detached, disconnected and, in some cases, desperate. I must in this instance address the spirit of these people to treat their physical pain.

There is a way of treating patients through Five Elements Acupuncture that is rooted in shamanism. It holds the notion that demons and earthbound spirits and entities can invade and take possession of a living person causing, at times, great distress. This can be deemed metaphoric, and the more modern-day approach is that a person has become so overtaken by their own emotional distress that they can no longer function in a healthy manner. Whatever your beliefs, this treatment feels sacred and profound and works by clearing enough distress out of the system to allow the person's spirit to once more take charge of their life.

The positioning of the needles seems to my mind, to create a funnel of light that clears away any invading spirits, emotions and other energies that are conflicting with the growth and progression of a person and masking their authentic self. By clearing the way, you could say 'casting out', and then introducing a positive flow of qi, or light force, the inner landscape changes, the spirit of the patient is able to return, and on some occasions, what has been, in some cases, almost unbearable pain vanishes overnight. It works wonders and, if appropriate, can be a life-changing treatment. Once the spirit is back in charge, rather than the distress, balance and health are able to return.

I remember a patient who came to me suffering from extremely distressing back pain. In his words, he has 'tried everything', from medical intervention in the form of painkilling medication and physiotherapy to massage etc. This man was in his mid-thirties, generally fit and healthy, but his back pain was taking over his daily life. He had recently separated from his wife and was feeling displaced and depressed. There was something about him that made me feel as though he had become 'possessed' by the trauma of the ending of his marriage, and that this extreme distress had become physical in nature, affecting his spine, which is the central support system of the body.

I decided to perform the treatment as described above, and the pain, seemingly miraculously, began to subside within moments. He left my clinic feeling more comfortable, but contacted me the next day saying, "I don't know what you've done, but I now have no pain!" Naturally, he was delighted, and the next couple of treatments were just to reinforce what had already taken place. This system of treatment which is prepared to look beyond the symptoms and towards the real level of distress is profoundly moving and can prove to be extremely helpful. I have a deep regard for this deeply healing ancient way, which begins the process of the reweaving of the level of the person that has been torn, broken or compromised in some way, usually from deep emotional pain.

Lighter Flows

I am reflected in the whole,
And the whole is reflected in
me.

As healing takes place, and creative change occurs, the flows of qi become higher, lighter and more refined. In the classical teachings of Five Elements, the higher gifts are gifts of the spirit and are called the virtues, or graces, and it is through these higher energetic resonance that we become awakened into a more elevated state of consciousness, which I think of as the trajectory of the soul.

The Graces of the Elements

Water moves through the emotion of fear towards the grace of wisdom.

Wood moves through the emotion of anger to the grace of benevolence.

Fire moves through the emotion of joy to the grace of unconditional and impersonal love.

Earth moves through the emotion of worry to the grace of compassion.

Metal moves through the emotion of grief to the grace of courage.

The elemental archetype appears to be tailor-made to each person's needs and emerges from a certain frequency of energy. Life is experienced according to the quality and character of this energy, and it is through this frequency that a soul incarnates into life, creating the gifts, challenges and blessings of this life span. We can all begin to know ourselves on an emotional level, but also acknowledge that we don't need to become stuck there but can give ourselves the freedom to move and dance more freely with the currents of life.

Whatever happens in life can be viewed from the perspective of getting to know yourself a little better. Over time, and with experience, whether slowly or quickly, you begin to learn how you we react and respond to different situations, and through this learn how you habitually engage with life and with people. You may now become familiar with your own shape, and with what you do when life throws a challenge your way, or someone or something upsets you. This knowledge gives you a certain level of power, because it enables you realise that you are free to make more choices over how to react and respond. You may possibly be tired of feeling angry, sad, victimised, misunderstood etc. and may choose to feel and respond differently next time the opportunity presents itself. You may instead choose humour, or choose to brush over whatever it is, or choose compassion, or to walk away or to speak out etc. Simply having the knowledge that you have choice begins a change and with that a sense of freedom. It is through the details of life, such as this, that enormous changes can evolve, and the gaining a level of charge or even mastery over personal responses can begin to take place.

Choice, which can also be called freewill, is a wonderful thing, and it took me years to realise that I had this power within me. The most useful thing we can do for ourselves is to know ourselves and through this knowing begin to grow and to bring about positive changes, happier results and healthier lives. In acupuncture terms, lack of growth and movement creates a state of stasis and stagnation, whereas positive growth creates good health and wellbeing.

At some point, you begin to realise that you have a responsibility for the levels of qi that you create within your being, and that dense and dark emotional states recreate dense and dark qi, and light and refined levels of being recreate light and refined flows of qi. The denser emotional states tend to emerge from deeply personal experience and hurt, which recreates itself in these tightened spheres. We believe in this phase of flow, that our own experience is unique to ourselves and because of this are unable to move through and beyond. As the view becomes broader, we realise that what we have encountered, many others have also encountered, and now the perception begins to understand that our experience is less personal and more shared. There is nothing that one person has experienced that has not been experienced by others. The trick is to find your way out of these dense shadowlands and into a higher perception where life is more shared and impersonal. As you rise higher, life becomes even less personal, and about 'me', and more about 'us' as growing and evolving people.

Life now takes on a whole new look, becoming finer and higher in frequency. It becomes easier to live in this field, as you discover that you are no longer grappling with heavy or dense forces. We are all earth beings and can share in the grace of compassion, as the spirit of the earth element. Compassion elevates the vision from 'self' to 'all'. Earth has a particular importance amongst the elements, being the force that manifests and that holds our presence in this world.

To hold this world in compassion, and all the people who live here, is to create a deep and powerful healing force. When viewed from the level of soul and the light of compassion, life takes on a different and expanded view, and difficulties transform into possibility for change and growth, creating the potential for new and lighter pathways.

The soul incarnates
so that it can know and resolve
what cannot be experienced in
the non-material planes
and, through these experiences,
it has the opportunity to reshape itself
and flow
towards positive change
and higher service to life.

Become authentic and enjoy the uncovering and discovery of who you really are, free from the bonds and bindings of conditioning and free from your masks of pain. Learn to be fully yourself and to hold yourself in a state of balanced equilibrium, no matter what (a quality of the earth element). To deeply accept yourself is a state of grace where you can also deeply accept other people. The lower self seeks to change people, and to separate and divide, into good, bad, better, worse, more than, less than. Taken from this view, none of us can ever quite measure up. But the soul accepts freely, loosening the constrictions of the lower forces. Its natural state is to flow loving compassion creating resonances of healing and harmony to all in its sphere of influence.

Chapter 2
The Hun Spirit of Wood

Attunement Meditation

The Creative Spirit of Spring

The river of life flows into ancient woodland, place of mystery and dreaming,
alive with nature spirits, and beings of the imagination.
You are here, and yet you are not. Coming and going as a dream.
What is real and what imagined?
There are many paths. Which to choose?
You are the spirit of the imagination, as vaporous as drifting clouds and as
mighty as the oak. You are the greening, the final push, as with the decision to
be, you burst through upon this plane with dynamic beauty and power.
Your essence is to create. Like an artist, you paint the barren landscape with a
loveliness that none can ignore or deny.
Shocking is the sudden thrust of winter into spring, and the desire that rises in
each of us to emulate you, to capture something of your spirit as we yearn to
flow with the sap of birthing dreams. You rise within each of us as an
impatience, an urgency. 'Now is the time,' you urge. 'Now is the moment to
stand strong and rooted. Now the moment of realisation of self as an
individuated spark of divinity. What will I do? How will I be?'
Your own spirit of adventure answers the call, questions tumbling, spilling
upon your palette. So many colours, textures from which to choose.

What to do?

How to express myself in life?

And so you root yourself deeply and naturally into the flows.

And as your roots grow downwards into the richness of your earthlife, you see that there are no barriers between your own precious life and the life of your imagined dreams.

The Hun Spirit of the Wood Element

Spirit of Creative Becoming

Spring is the pure spirit of the birthing of life, creativity and the arena of the imagination. The hun is the name given by Five Element theory to this spirit, which is said to be the spirit of the ethereal soul, who lives in the ethers of the imagination. The hun are the spirits of the natural world whose task is to dream the power and beauty of nature from the ethereal and into the materialised realms of earth. They impel each of us an individual and dynamic spirit of nature to use this same power and beauty to dream our own creative impulses into life. The hun are vital and immediate. What is it that you have come to earth to 'do', to 'be', 'to share' to 'gift', to 'learn and discover'? The hun help us to define ourselves as individual, creating the impulse within each of us to discover purpose and artistry in our lives, impelling each one of us to stretch and reach higher and wider towards the fulfilment of our own blueprint of who we really are. There is a dynamism in the hun, which prompts individual growth through imagination, hope, action, vitality and movement.

Who would you be if there were no limits?

The Essence of Wood Power

The essence of power of the wood element is to surge with an unstoppable passion to reach for your goals, to stretch to uncover more of your essential being. To push down into the earth and to rise mightily towards the bright sunlight of your highest potential. Yours is the self-belief and yours, the creative imagination. When these two passions join forces, you become unstoppable.

The Harmonious
Resonance of Wood

Season is spring.

Colour is green.

Sound is a shout of youth and vigour, the shout that gives birth to conscious awareness and waking up.

Aroma is fresh rising and 'zesty'.

In the body, the wood element governs the liver, gallbladder, connective tissues and eyesight,

The qualities invoked by wood are kindness, hope, rebirth, dynamism, motivation, assertiveness, artistry, vision and planning and the action needed to see something to fruition.

The Disharmonious
Resonance of Wood

Anger, frustration irritation overly assertive, lack of vision – 'can't see the wood for the trees'. Lack of action and motivation. Rigid thinking and beliefs overly competitive.

Symptoms – Migraines and headaches, issues arising from stress, insomnia, PMS, ME and chronic fatigue, addictions, gallbladder symptoms and gallstones, overly tight or lax ligaments, issues around sexual organs and fertility, sciatica, arthritis.

Awakening into Higher Consciousness

(The Ethereal Soul)

Benevolence that sees each life form as an individual, each with their own blueprint to follow, to emerge as a higher expression, and but also as an integral and essential part of the part of the Divine Plan.

Song of the Wood Element

The Green Dragon of the East emerges, mighty,
glorious and beautiful.

She roars her fiery breath into the March winds,
awakening even the most dormant into activity.

She is ancient, she is mythological, a potent symbol of hope,
fertility and rebirth.

Her call is to action.

Her challenge, to dream of higher purpose, and her awakening is of the consciousness, the power of the imagination in you, to ignite hope of change, growth and renewal.

Spring
Season of Wood

After the hidden, closed and quiet yin of winter, the qi changes and begins a rapid and surging ascent into yang. Just when we thought we couldn't take the sinking dreariness of winter dragging its heels, along comes a potent awakening and spring appears! As if impatient to express itself, in it rushes, upwards and outwards, drawing with it new growth and flourishes of colour with which to paint over the drabness of late winter terrain.

This vigorous burst of rising yang stimulates enormous activity, and nature is all of a sudden busy in its efforts to recreate itself and bring something to life. Spring is the phase in the year when growth is powerful, vigorous, compelling, and alive with new beginnings. Noisy with activity, the sap is rising, a perfect time to freshen up mind, body and spirit with new horizons and adventure. Who has not yearned for the freshness and warmth of spring to bring you out of closed winter closets and melt away those 'winter blues'?

Life bursts forwards and upwards with a shout of excitement from every hedgerow and crevice, from every piece of ground and every tree. It all about 'now'. Now is the time to dust off the mental cobwebs and spring-clean the body, now is the time for action and now the time for something different, maybe something new and long dreamt of?

The artistry of nature and her spirits abound, and the landscape is rapidly transformed with magical colour and beauty. Spring is exciting, alive with movement and clamouring with noisy activity. Green is everywhere. New shoots, leaves and fresh bright grasses. Green is the colour of birthing, of magic and of hope. Spring is a signal to start again. It wipes the slate of the old year clean, birthing a fresh new wave of hope and purpose. Colour appears overnight in gardens, and sunlight and warmth sink into hungry, aching winter bodies. Wood qi stimulates a rapid ascent of energy in people, bringing with it an immediacy and fuelling the ability to envision, plan and organise.

The wood function of qi, which can be thought of as 'consciousness', is imperative for the overall wellbeing of a person and the spirit of an individual life. Planning, organisation and regeneration are at the heart of the success and continuation of all living organisms. This level of intricacy is also to be seen at the core of every process in the human body. Each function and process exists in its own right, but the real magnificence is in the consciousness that stimulates all functions and processes to work together in true cooperation, in the creation of a healthy and balanced human being. These dynamics of stimulation and cooperation can be seen echoing throughout an individual in the creation and then the fulfilment of hopes, dreams and aspirations needed for physical, mental, emotional and spiritual wellbeing. In practical terms, the body needs movement which will help to cleanse and clear the stagnation of winter dormancy. Try taking 'it's great to be alive!' walks in nature amongst the vital green growth. Take the time to look at what is happening, and see if you can feel the awakening around you? Can you feel a stirring within? This will help towards balancing and aligning you with the forces of spring, helping to activate ideas and potential that may have lain dusty and dormant through the winter months.

How the Wood Element Arises in the Body

In the body, the element wood governs action, movement and flexibility, arising in the physicality through the connective tissues, the liver and gallbladder and the eyes. The gallbladder meridian surfaces at the temple and zigzags around the side of the head, before descending down the sides of the torso and hips. It then makes its careful way down the outsides of the legs and feet, ending at the nail of the fourth toe. Its zigzagging course echoes the nature of the gallbladder, whose gift is movement and the vision to consider all eventualities before arriving at a detailed and precise plan. Chinese medicine tells us that the gallbladder oversees the eyes and the ability to focus physically, mentally or emotionally.

The liver meridian begins at the big toe, rises up the inside of the legs, around the genital area and abdomen, extending to the middle of the rib cage. The route of this meridian indicates the vital role that the liver qi plays in reproductive health. Points along this channel are frequently used in the treatment of PMS and fertility issues. The liver is a vital component of the reproductive cycle, being responsible both for the storing of blood during rest and the release of the blood required for physical activity and during the menstrual cycle. This process requires the precision, planning and action that is the keynote of the element wood.

The final acupuncture point along the liver meridian is wonderfully named 'Gate of Hope' and can be a powerful reminder of hope as the herald of growth, rebirth and the adventure that comes from exploring more expanded and newer states of being. I often use this point in treatment to free a person who has become overly burdened or 'stuck' in their life or in their emotional state and is unable to see a way forward. It can bring in a new wave of qi, helping to raise the energy and the vision to see what is needed once more.

The 'Gate of Hope' is to be found in ribcage at the front of the chest. It is situated in the region of both the heart and the lungs, indicating the importance of the coming together of these different aspects of self to create that state of being that is hope. This point brings together the fiery joy of the heart (fire element) with the inspiration of the breath (metal element) with the potency of the creative power of direction (wood element). The coming together of these forces brings about the powerful light of hope. We can now see where we are going and how and why we are going there. This point is a good illustration of how the elements come together in support of each other. By invoking the qi of these three elements, a gateway can open into your next step in life. Inspiration, joy and direction are the key words here. Without the light of hope, life can become drab, mundane and pointless. It is up to us to continue to create our own avenues of purpose until such a time as a higher purpose, or a calling of the soul or higher consciousness may become evident.

In my own experience, it can be difficult to continue to move forwards creatively when the light of hope is at a low ebb. When this happens, take a little time to remember why you set out on the path that you are currently following, or the project that you are engaged in. Try to establish where you are in terms of achieving your original goal, and, if need be, re-establish your motivation? Why am I doing what I'm doing? What is my desired outcome? These are questions to pose to yourself periodically to keep your vision awake and engaged. There is nothing worse than setting out on a certain pathway and then becoming distracted, despairing and, ultimately, demotivated. This collapses the all-important wood qi and can lead to the depression of a loss of direction.

In my own case, my children have been the motivating force, both in terms of providing for them materially, but perhaps, more importantly, showing them that it is possible to find a way through challenges, sometimes against all odds. We may all encounter times in life that seem so beset with difficulties that it's hard to see the wood for the trees. At these times, find yourself a symbol, and call it 'hope'. It could be a beautiful stone that you keep close to you, a message that you post in a prominent position, a symbol such as a star beaming out light, a healthy plant growing and flourishing towards the light, a religious or spiritual icon, or a prayer. There are many ideas that could be helpful, but it is important to know what will work for you. Use your symbol as a ray of light to carry you at the times when you cannot carry yourself.

I move through
the dark forest of difficulties
with hope as my guide.
The ray of hope illuminates my way,
casting light on all obstacles
and melting them away.
The beauty of my true path awaits
my presence.

The ability to envision, plan, organise and carry through, together with the flexibility to adapt and change are the gifts of a healthy wood element. Rigidity of mind, body and spirit can manifest if plans and personal perspectives, goals and aspirations are too formal or firmly fixed, not allowing for further expansion or growth. If you're not flexible enough, then you may become brittle and 'broken'. There is also a danger of being overly flexible in a way that enables other people to fulfil their own dreams but compromises yourself.

'Woody' folks are often highly charged and highly creative. They may be long and 'sinewy' in build, or solid and 'square' in shape. The feet often have a 'squared off' look to them, and the shoulders can be pronounced, also having a rather 'square' look about them. The voice comes up and out like a 'shout' and is clearly defined and assertive. The wood element likes to be in charge and in control, being a natural and strong leader. There can be a stiffness about the neck and shoulders as ideas become blocked somewhere between the dreaming of them (in the head) and putting them into action (in the body). Stiffness can also arise through rigid thoughts and the need to be 'right'. This can create a certain rigidity in the body as attitudes become inflexible.

Try liberating yourself by being 'wrong' sometimes, or by not needing to have the last word in a dispute, it's such a relief! Try not to mind whether you are right or wrong, but to see life with a higher and clearer vision. There is a Chinese wisdom saying, 'Who knows what is right and what is wrong?' What appears to be right at one time can change, as can what appears to be wrong. Perhaps 'right and wrong' are just not necessary in every argument? Wood qi asks that you extend your vision and perception to view life from different angles and points of view.

Migraines and headaches can be symptomatic of an imbalance in the wood element, as the qi becomes tight and blocked through strong emotions and frustrations. Migraines can be linked to problems with the sight and can also appear prior to or with the onset of menstruation, both of which are indications of an imbalance in the flows of wood qi.

On the face, a greenish shade emerges in the complexion, particularly noticeable around the eyes and mouth, or sometimes visible as a hovering hue above and around the surface of the face. Conditions such as arthritis, neck pain, PMS and gout can arise from the frustrations and anger of thwarted goals, rigid beliefs, inflexible attitudes, or from the inability to express emotions in a creative, healthy and energising way.

At the other end of the scale, a kind of lax apathy can emerge in a person whose wood qi is low or 'deficient'. Here we find little ability to 'see' a future, to envision, dream, set goals or have much in the way of personal aspiration. Dreams stay as dreams, and there is often not enough of the practical energy needed to galvanise dreams into fruition. These people can appear hazy as if out of focus, often talking about what they intend to do, but very rarely taking the steps necessary to achieve whatever it is, appearing listless and vague, unable to 'root' into an effective and fulfilling life.

Wood governs the eyes. The eyes are the portals to the soul. To look deeply into a person's eyes is to know them at a soul level. Take a moment to stand in front of a mirror and gaze into your own eyes. Who do you see looking back at you? Look deeply into the eyes of those you love, taking the time to see who looks back at you? Some people are comfortable with this level of intimacy and some are not. Sometimes people are unable to make direct eye contact, as if wanting to remain hidden. On a physical level, a healthy diet rich in green vegetables will help to ensure the physical eyes keep in sharp and clear focus, while on a soul level, a healthy inner life, rich with ideas dreams and imagination will help to strengthen the inner vision.

The Hun Spirit of Spring

Can You Wake Up and Rise Out of Your Sleep?

With the rising of the creative hun forces of spring, energy returns to the landscape, stretching and flexing as if waking from a deep sleep. Although growth is rising, and rapidly tumbling out of every nook and cranny, each life form is nevertheless consistent with nature's plan, following the blueprint already laid down by a higher hand. The result, far from being chaotic, is ordered, balanced and beautiful. Bare branches are strung with hazy blossoms and as if by magic daffodils appear, seemingly from nowhere. This blueprint resides in the invisible etheric realms and governs the growth and expression of every living thing. The hun inhabit the vaporous nature of the dreams and imagination. They plant the seeds of growth and oversee the planning and organisation that results in germination and flourishing. They are the nature spirits, fairies and beautiful beings of the imaginary realms.

The hun can speak through sleep and dreamtime and inspire creativity through the beauty of living phenomena. They plant seeds of ideas in the barren landscapes of the mind and, through their magical ways, fuel the imagination needed to bring the seeds to life. They are said to live in the vaporous clouds and shafts of sunlight, coming and going between earth and the etheric realms. They are the messengers whose task is to create and to fulfil the blueprint of a higher intelligence.

Life has a very precise order, each season following on from the last and each life form, whether plant, animal or mineral, having a particular part to play in the support and creation of the whole. This sense of order is overseen by the hun. Each creature, plant, flower or tree has its own etheric nature and must follow its own blueprint, remaining true to itself and its own fulfilment. An oak tree can never become a bluebell, or an apple become a peach or a swan. Every form has its own unique role to fulfil in the intricate and self-sustaining pattern of life. So it is with people. Each person has their own path to follow and their own unique contribution to make to the intricate and self-perpetuating pattern of humanity.

The hun are seen as the spirits of the ethereal soul, which create the patterns of life and enliven a person with consciousness. According to Chinese medicine, they are housed in the liver and are concerned with rest and movement both though the physical body and through thoughts, emotions and the higher realms of creativity and imagination. Both too much movement and too little movement disturb the harmonious flows of this aspect of self. The hun teach of the order of both rest and movement, dreaming and practical action. They bring these seeming opposites together through the activation of conscious choice and awareness. The inability to move very much, to stretch, to extend the body, thoughts and imagination beyond a narrow parameter are indications of a restriction of the hun. At the other end of the scale, over extending, an overactive imagination and constant movement with no rest are also indicative of imbalance.

In balance, the wood element oversees the etheric nature of the soul path, the blueprint of the individual, ordered, balanced and beautiful. It invokes the vision and imagination needed first to know, and then to create your own destiny. Without the motivation and planning needed to follow a path, even the greatest hopes, dreams and aspirations will come to nothing, remaining untouched and undiscovered in the realms of dreaming and fantasy.

A key resonance of wood is the dynamism and motivation needed to grow fully into your own highest potential, igniting the magnificent Green Dragon of your dreams.

The hun spirits as the keepers of dreams, bring the energy and awakening of pure vision down from the sphere of fantasy and imagination into the everyday, and the conscious awareness, creating the hope of something coming to fruition, perhaps something new, or different? The ability to envision is the orbit of all great artists, creators, inventors and those who can 'see' beyond the ordinary and mundane.

Here is also to be found the gift of prophecy and clairvoyance and is the realm of healers and shamans and those with extraordinary, in other words, beyond ordinary, vision. This level of vision requires a 'flexibility' in terms of what is 'real' and what imagined. The gift of flexibility from the level of the physical body, through emotional and mental attitudes and beyond, is attributed to the element wood.

The wood element is youthful (childish) and exuberant. It is important not to lose sight of this nature within yourself. Don't forget how to play, because playing stimulates the imagination giving flight to new ideas. Remember how as a child, your flights of fancy built your games into ones of adventure and imagination? What were your favourite games? Do you still carry these threads into your more adult world?

How motivated are you as a growing and awakening individual?

To grow, to extend, to expand?
To reach higher and deeper and wider into the essence of who you are?
Have a good stretch.
Enjoy the awakening of your tissues.
Breathe fully and deeply, feeling your spirits rise up and your body enliven.
Enjoy the feeling of being alive!
Now is your time to be here, and to be fully present in your own life.
Now is your opportunity to dream and then to root your visions, reaching high,
and then bringing them down from the realms of fantasy to the realms of being.
Now is the time.
Ask yourself
'Who Am I?'
'What is it that I have always seen my self
Doing?
Being?
Having?
Creating?
Giving?'
Say these words out loud –
'I am the author and artist of my own way. The path ahead of me goes around,
above and below all the obstacles it encounters, transforming them into the
textures, the colours and contours of a life well lived.'

Take time to really feel and experience the power of these words echoing through you. Allow the vision of your awakened self to flow to your highest and deepest extremities. Give time and space for the feelings of awakening to take root deeply within you. Allow the space for this to flourish throughout your life as a new and empowered version of you.

From this space of creative potential, feel the higher essences of hope, joy and gratitude arising within you and giving life and substance to your dreams. Give thanks for all that is now arising and for every blessing that is coming your way through these visions of the new you.

Give space for this in your life, in your thoughts and in your feelings.

Anger – Emotion of Wood

The Creative Force of Movement and Change

The energy of 'anger' in Chinese Medicine, refers more accurately to the impulse and motivation needed to change, express or to move forwards with a thrust of energy. Lack of movement could be thought of as lack of anger, potentially leading to the 'stagnation' of natural forces. Life can become very dreary if the natural flows and vibrancy of spring qi are denied or suppressed. Movements of energy inside a person are 'energies in motion', or emotions. Wood governs emotional responses and the appropriate storing and releasing of these responses and reactions. We are emotional beings, and it is perhaps this aspect more than any other, that creates our humanity. As we create our own and individual emotional responses, we can respond to the emotions in other people, creating a sense of commonality.

We have all at some time been overwhelmed by powerful emotions, which can build and create, or can devastate and destroy, so strong is the power of their movement. Some people are adept at hiding, compressing and oppressing their emotions. Others are only too happy to express them without regard for the consequences. If emotions are concerned with 'energy in motion', it easy to guess what may happen if the energy doesn't move or becomes 'stuck', compressed or somehow compacted within the emotional arena of a person. This emotion then takes a hidden, but potent and potentially toxic, centre stage as it longs for expression and movement. We may keep revisiting it again, again and again as it seeks release and resolution. It may become so habitual we somehow think that this emotion is 'us'! For example, "I'm always like this: angry/depressed/tearful/jealous…"

The perfect manifestation of wood qi is to feel each emotion with a deep intensity as it arises and then to facilitate its conscious and expressive free flow through the mind and body. By not denying or suppressing your feelings, you rather welcome both the arising and, then after full and conscious expression, the receding.

Chinese wisdom uses the image of the strong forces of weather to describe a healthy way of managing and understanding your emotional state. Much like a mighty storm, the emotion rises to a zenith, and this is when it is at its most potent, powerful and potentially creative or destructive. Then comes the next phase of falling away and the dwindling as, having run its course, the storm then blows itself out again, and peace returns once more. This image shows the progression of both movement and stillness – appropriate action and expression, followed by rest. Think of powerful winds blowing with tremendous power through a forest. They run their course, reach their zenith, before dying back again without causing major damage to the trees. It is viewed as healthy and appropriate to feel and to express emotion, but then to let the movement die away naturally before damage is inflicted on self or other people. The force is consciously experienced and acknowledged.

I welcome my own rising anger as a creative and generating force of my own empowerment.
I do not use it against others, but to clear my own vision and my own path and to activate my
internal creative artist

A level of flexibility is needed to both flow with and to withstand the intensity of strong movements of energy, without collapsing under the force. The image of bamboo is honoured as a healthy expression of wood qi. It is incredibly strong, adaptable and prolific but has the flexibility to bend to any conditions without losing its own shape or integrity.

Emotions teach us as individuals, something about who we are and how we react to life in all its flows of exaltation, joy, frustrations and challenges. Too many powerful emotions are exhausting for the wood energy, potentially leading towards depression, stress, lack of wellbeing and arising as physical symptoms as indication of distress. To regain a sense of equanimity, a conscious attempt to gain a more 'level-headed' approach to life's ups and down may be called for. If your internal landscape is too stormy, nothing can really grow or take shape as the forces of your creativity are overly absorbed in weathering the storms of life. It may be time to reign in any destructive forces in favour of the more creative ways of dealing with pressures as they emerge. Repeated cycles of powerful emotions can drain and disperse your creative spirit.

For good health, a balanced approach is advocated, where emotions are neither oppressed nor overly indulged, but are useful as a means of creative expression and as a gateway to a deeper knowledge of self as a moving and dynamic expression of consciousness.

Are you predictable and habitual in your emotional responses?

Are you unpredictable and stormy?
Are you controlled and restrictive?
Are you fresh, alive and responsive?

Wood Element as Visionary

Visionaries, shamans and seers have strongly developed wood qi (energy). Their strength lies in an ability to 'see' (intuit, foretell) what is not easily visible to other people. Their vision extends beyond the ordinary into higher and more creative realms, offering insights and perceptions that are not generally accessible in an everyday sense. The vision can extend with a piercing clarity into events and situations, past present and future, bringing a lucidity that of itself can seem exceptional. This is the realm of clairvoyance, and this level of vision can bring healing when a pathway out of and beyond a difficult or hazardous situation is sought. The gift of clairvoyance is a grace of the hun spirits, and appears magical, as the vision is lifted to higher realms above the grey of clouded thinking and up to the blue sky of unclouded thoughts. From this higher perspective, life can take on a new simplicity as difficulties and disharmonies fall from sight, and answers that were hitherto not visible can become apparent.

On occasion, I am able to 'see' into people at times in a way that defies rational explanation, often able to look deeply into their energetic matrix as a way of moving blocks in qi and bringing about healing. Visions and images often appear to me that defy explanation in an everyday sense but bring useful information about the energetic and spiritual health of the person I am treating. A close friend of mine can 'see' people's past lives with an incredible clarity, again something that defies explanation in a rational sense.

Many people want to know about their future or the answer to taxing problems and seek the support of a clairvoyant or the help of some tools of divination, such as tarot cards or dowsing. This can prove helpful at times and can help to deepen your conscious awareness of yourself, but caution should be taken not to become overly dependent on these influences but to seek your own inner vision wherever possible.

Meditation
To Clear Your Inner Vision

Sit comfortably and upright, relaxing the body and gently closing the eyes to close down the external vision, allowing all concerns of your day to softly fade from your mind.

The Pure Light of Creative Power – Imagine a spark of white light deep within your abdomen. See it extending to become a beautiful sphere of white light which encompasses your lower body in its glow.

The Pure Light of the Peaceful Heart – Imagine now, a spark of light within the centre of your chest. See it extending to become a beautiful sphere of white light which encompasses your whole upper body in its glow.

The Pure Light of Vision – Imagine now, a spark of light within the centre of your head. See it extending to become a beautiful sphere of white light which encompasses your whole head in its glow.

Try to balance all three spheres of light in your awareness.

Then focus on the sphere of light illuminating your head and enjoy resting your busy mind for a while in the pure light of your peaceful mind.

When you are ready, begin to shrink each sphere of light in turn, returning it to a small spark in the centre of your head, your head and your abdomen. Begin with your head, and then your heart and lastly your abdomen.

You will feel fresh and alive, and if practiced regularly for a few minutes, this meditation will help to clear your inner vision and sharpen your focus.

The Wood Element out of Balance

When Stress Takes Root

Problems, challenges, frustrations and obstacles arise, when the vision becomes clouded, emotions are not expressed appropriately, and the resulting inner confusion takes root. Internal movements of qi become compromised as thoughts and feelings seek an outlet. Some people become prone to regular 'outbursts'. They may feel irritated or constantly stressed, feeling that life itself is obstructing their very progress. "There are too many demands," they cry. "Too much to do, and too little time to do it!" Life is rubbing up against them, causing constant friction and irritation. These people are always on the go, with a propensity to setting themselves unrealistic goals, becoming frustrated, angry and distressed when they can't meet them. It's stress all the way!

Stress, in the case of wood qi, is a reaction to perceived obstacles and to impeded progress. The obstacle may be perceived as lack of time, but in reality, is most likely to be due to the inability to manage time, and much effort can be wasted trying to 'cram too much in'. It might be a reaction to other people. If you have a strong wood element in your makeup, you may have a strong desire to 'control', and dislike other people having the upper hand. You may feel 'pot bound' as your roots coil round and round in tangling circles, with not enough room to facilitate your natural growth and creating ever tightening loops of stress and frustration. You long to be free to grow and to thrive in your own and very individual way.

There is a different level of stress which may arise, and is what my father used to call, 'the stress of not doing'. You may have too much time on your hands and life feels vague and unsatisfactory. You know that there is 'something' out there, but you can't find the motivation to reach for it. This is most definitely a call to claim and take charge of your life and your own creative destiny. It may be that your internal focus is too easily diverted, and is an indication that focus needs to become more sustained and directed, which in turn will help you to 'root down' into your own sense of self and the life that you are beginning to realise that you can create.

People with a highly charged wood element can be prone to stress in many different forms. It is vital for the overall health to find ways that help to alleviate this and relieve the body and mind of some of the pressure placed upon it by undue or habitual stress. All the meditation and visualisation exercises in this book are ways in which to engage the senses and to remove them from the strains of the everyday world, providing a different, and perhaps more creative, perspective. If you are stressed, try to create some options and ideas. Are you stressed by home, by work, by life in general? Then allow your creative imagination to help you to find a different way. Stress can be indicative of the need for the creative processes to become more activated, as stress creates a feeling of deadlock. What can you do to release the deadlock? Learning to release frustration through physical activity can be helpful. When my very busy life threated to overpower me, I used to just pull my running shoes on and bolt out of the door, even if only for a few minutes. It always helped. Walking can be a very good way of getting mind and body back into alignment and of organising thoughts and feelings.

Wood energy is all about action, and action helps to create movement, which as we have seen, is the keynote of creativity and emotional expression. Movement can focus around the body but can also encompass other dimensions of life. What movements do you need to create on an emotional level? Are you being asked to consider greater movements such as relocation, changing your career path or avenue of employment? Do you need to refocus your mental attitudes and beliefs that may have become restrictive, outgrown or rigid? Stress is an indication that something needs to move, either physically, emotionally, mentally or spiritually.

Allow yourself the space in your life, which stress usually deprives you of. Stress is so immediate and demanding. What would happen if you were to go beyond the stress and to take hold of it so that it no longer holds sway as a habitual reaction?

The following mental exercise engages and stimulates the imagination, helping to remove you from your everyday day concerns, introducing a new element of creativity.

Tree Meditation

Imagine that you are your favourite tree.

What do you look like?

Take some time to observe your tree-self in detail. Are you a sapling, or fully grown? Are you timeless and ancient or fresh and young?

Do you stand alone in the landscape, or are you set amongst others, perhaps in a small copse, a garden, wild woodland or forest.

How does your trunk feel to the touch?

Is it smooth like skin, or rugged and pitted with time? What does your tree tell you about yourself?

How is the weather around you? Can you feel gentle breezes paying with your fluttering leaves, or the warm sunshine shafting its rays through your strong and pliable branches?

Can you hear drops of rain tumbling through and around you, quenching your thirsty roots?

Taking a full and slow deep breath, and feel your tree, tracing the course of your mighty roots deep down into the fragrant soil.

Follow the roots as they make their way through and around obstacles, stones, rocks, man-made structures…

They forge their route deep into the earth, and there they stay, growing and sinking deeper with each new season's growth.

Feel the 'aliveness' of the rising sap as your tree comes to its springtime of new growth, shoots and leaves springing from bare branches.

Feel the exhilaration of your own new growth.

Moving into the Shadowlands of the Wood Element

Exploring the Hidden Depths That May Absorb Your Creative Power

There are times in life when anger arises as a valid response to events. Anger can be entirely appropriate when a person is under threat or attack, acting as a strong protector. Anger rises as a powerful force whose message is 'do something!'. It cannot be ignored as, like a thundering dragon, it tears its way through the feelings and the body as an urgent and intense instigator of action. These are appropriate and valid responses to threat.

However, difficulties arise when the dark dragon is always on call as a first resort, and anger becomes the habitual response to the ups and downs of life. Excess anger is the domain of an imbalance in the wood element. Whatever life throws at you, up comes the dark dragon, roaring and furious. You feel constantly angry, stressed, frustrated. This may be outwardly displayed or not, depending on your disposition. Some people may appear outwardly calm but harbour the dragon in the dark, caging intense emotions in their interior realms and not only placing the mind and the body under considerable strain, but absorbing energy that could be used in a more creative way and creating emotional and energetic stagnation.

In other people, the qi is very reactive, the dark dragon leaping and flying to the fore, with nothing hidden or kept under wraps. It's tension all the way, and as emotions build, it's difficult to keep a sense of vision and a clear perspective as the bands of stress tighten and blind you. Life can appear to be very restricted from this angle as stress breeds more stress and the emotions themselves can become part of a compulsive cycle. This too can place mind and body under considerable stress.

It is easy to turn to swift 'fixes', and a wood personality can also be an addictive one. At times of stress, the need for alcohol can rocket, revealing that not only is the element of wood distressed, but is also now coming under attack and shouting for help. Alcohol is acutely irritating to the liver, and too much alcohol, coupled with too much stress, can quickly set up a cycle of cravings, which as a long-term coping strategy can lead to profound addiction and serious health issues.

Detoxing, and shielding from too much alcohol, poor quality food and excessive emotions is really what your overly burdened wood element needs. Eating lots of green foods, 'zesty' with life force is a very good way of helping to support your liver. Choose fresh and organic fruits and vegetables where possible, with the understanding that you are ingesting the dynamic forces of nature! Find ways to give space to a more balanced and creative outlook and refocus your vision of how you wish your life to be. You will be repaid hugely as your sense of wellbeing improves, making you more relaxed and less reactive to stressful situations.

In people with a deficit in wood qi, the opposite end of the spectrum can be seen. Nothing galvanises them to anger or to a roused state of action, even at those times in life when anger may be a very appropriate response, they remain repressed and passive, never roused to action. They make be overly 'meek', or timid by nature, not feeling able to assert their individuality enough to allow their emotions and zest for life free reign. Any potential uprising of energy is swallowed down again, where it implodes internally and can potentially lead to states of depression. If wood qi is not allowed its natural expressing of uprising, or if its roots are not sufficiently deep, it can crash like a huge tree causing devastation to both tree and surrounding landscape, and this person can, like the trunk and branches of the fallen tree, feel 'broken'.

In the shadowlands, wood qi moves in tight circles, tense and constricted like a darkened forest. It may compensate for lack of creativity and lack of expression by creating rigid routines and habits. In the depths of the shadowy forest, the dark dragon yearns to be free, to soar and spread its creative wings. The deep frustration it feels tethers it into its darkened lair, where instead of writing its own vivid story of life, it harbours stories of anger and stress, using these to pit its frustration against the world.

Wood on the Rise

Reclaiming Yourself

In our culture, anger is often seen as a negative emotion. However, in its pure state, it is the energy of movement and change. In terms of the life of which we are all a part, a plant needs 'anger' to propel it into growth and expansion, and in people, it can be those white-hot moments of anger that become pivotal in creating change, thrusting a person towards a new direction. It is anger, that states, "That's enough! There's no going back." It's at those times that a fresh new phase of life is needed, as the old ways no longer 'fit' or enhance your personal growth. These are times of pure clear vision when you are compelled to shrug off the old and outworn and try something fresh, new, challenging. Wood qi is about challenge. Can you rise to meet challenge, or do you wither and fade in the face of it? How is your ability to plan and map your way towards your destiny? Can you see a clear route ahead?

A birthing mother needs the spirit of anger to propel her infant into life and then to protect and safeguard its growth. This same energy gives rise to other phases of power, as ideas and plans are gestated and birthed into life. Here is the energy you need, and now is the time to harness it. In its pure state, anger is the supreme motivation to shout 'Yes!' and to claim the power of your own being and your own growth. The power of the hun spirit is the power that you must claim within yourself to say, or to shout, 'Yes!' to your own shape, your own blueprint, and 'Yes!' to fulfilling your own higher, wider and deeper potential. If 'Yes!' is the word that gives life, then 'No' is the word that safeguards your own power in the face of threat.

'Yes and No'
as Clear Words of Power

Please take some time in your own quiet space to consider the power of these two small words. They are two of the smallest words in our language, but in essence they have the most power. In these words, there is no compromise.
They are complete within themselves.
How do you use the power of 'Yes' and 'No' in your own life?
Do you use it for control or for creativity?
Do you say one when you really mean the other?

Spirit as Artist

After the exhausting dreariness of late winter, in come the rising patterns of qi. Out with the old and in with the new! The hun spirits will urge you to detox your body of winter warmer foods that have left you feeling tired and sluggish, and this same call will galvanise you into spring cleaning and decluttering. It will give you the impetus to freshen up your environment, perhaps at home and at work, and to freshen up your internal emotional environment. In terms of the hun, clutter represents the outworn and the past and will gather stagnant qi. The hun create movement and change. Lack of movement produces stagnation which is death to the creative spirit.

In nature, nothing is fixed, nothing static and nothing unchangeable or immovable. Even the mightiest mountain is affected by and subjected to erosion by external conditions. In the same way, none of us are fixed, and our lives are anything but static or unchangeable. How much better to have the artistry and foresight to make the changes you want in your life, rather than simply letting life 'happen' to you? The qi of wood urges just this, with a cry of 'now is the time', it prompts you into envisioning your dreams and bringing them to life.

The following is a Dream Visioning exercise. It may prompt your imagination to take flight. All creative impulses come through thoughts and imagination. Everything that we manifest or creates begins here, and we have the power to say yes to it and create something wonderful, or to say no and let the dreams fade.

Dream Visioning

Please take some time to consider your life as it is now.
Think about how your life is, your relationships, your working and home life,
friendships and everything else that makes up your life.
If it was a natural landscape, what would it look like?
Would it be alive with colour and beauty, or would it be somewhat drab and
devoid of colour? Would it include people, and places, or would it be solitary?
What time of year is it in your landscape, what time of day? Does this reflect
your spirit?
Is it contained, or is it expansive with big views and distant horizons? Would
you like to change it? How would you really like it to be?
Listen for a while to the whisperings of your dreams.
Give them space to come to you, meandering through the everyday thoughts,
bringing the magic of inspiration.
What do they tell you?
What is it that you really want?
You may like to make some notes, or if you are that way inclined, even paint or
draw.
Imagine that your new version of life is laid out in front of you.

How would you like it to look and what experiences, feelings, relationships, etc. would you like it to encompass?

Take time to muse, daydream, imagine…

When you have created the landscape of your dreams, visualise yourself standing there at the centre with your heart open and your arms outstretched claiming it all.

'Yes' comes straight from the heart.

It is already yours.

Feel the expansive feelings that flow through you as you claim it all and ask the spirits of your imagination to help you to make it real and to bring it into being.

Over the following days and weeks, take note of the promptings and take the action that is needed to ground and root these promptings into your life. This exercise may be repeated as need to encourage your spirits of imagination and change. Although there is a strong element of dreaming and imagination in the realm of the wood element, on the other side is seen the practical nature of making things real by planning and taking the steps to fulfil your goals and dreams.

The hun as spirits of creativity and the artistry, encourage this growth to awaken and to emerge in your life. The hun urge you to listen inwardly to your own creative flows and to allow space, time and energy for your internal creator to arise. Artistry can arise through learning to be creative with your mental, spiritual and emotional worlds, as its realm is not purely physical. It is the invoker of the imagination. Take up your brush and repaint your worn-out internal canvas with new colour and with new shapes and patterns. The hun are energetic and youthful, and like Peter Pan, regardless of your age in years, they will keep you young, lively in outlook and active in the talents and gifts that make up your life. The message of the hun is to wake up and to rise up with the growth of springtime to renewed vision. They are all about new beginnings as the herald to renewed personal growth.

There is something truly magical in daring to dream and there is also magic to be found in the strength of motivation needed to follow the promptings of your internal creator to design the pathway to making your dreams come true. Messages of 'be bold', 'dream big' are all around but that is only half the story. You will be faced with internal devastation and disappointment if you do not make the changes and follow the promptings that are designed to lead you from where you are now to where you would love to be in your own life. Dreaming of itself can be a blissful pastime as you muse the hours away, but without some degree of planning and activity, it is consigned to the realms of pure fantasy. Best not to further feelings of frustration provoking the 'Dark Dragon' to stir in its lair. "You told me to dream," it roars. Yes, but we also suggested that you venture out of the darkness of your own frustration, spreading your wings and lifting your sights to make your dreams come true.

In my own case, I had an idea to write some books a few years ago, and I was excitedly talking about them to friends and family and making some tentative inroads into creating them. As time went by, an uncomfortable realisation dawned that I was doing more talking about them than doing. There and then I made a vow to either write them or forget the whole thing! I vowed never to mention them again as idle chatter. It was becoming boring to me, and most likely to the people on the receiving end! I took hold of myself and this was just the internal motivation I needed. I got on with writing them. I was then lucky enough to find a publisher who was willing to publish them for me, and my dream came true. This was a salutary lesson in understanding that I was wasting much energy in idle dreaming and needed to focus my attention on doing what was needed.

Rising Higher

Into the Realms of Kindness and Growth

You may be trapped in a cycle of desperately 'wanting', but just unable to make it happen. Whatever you do simply doesn't propel you forwards. Deep feelings of inadequacy and impotence can arise, with a dreadful stagnation making its dreary way through your life. 'The moment' never quite arises and you live in the grips of all that is lacking. There is an expression 'lack of wood' in the acupuncture world, which describes a lack of creative power and lack of the motivation needed to do what you want to do and to be what you want to be. You become overridden by other people and other concerns and can never quite get to grips with your own self and your own life. Your own power seems to leak from your hands and your best laid plans get forgotten or put on hold for another time or another place.

People for whom this happens are often the kind ones who put other people and their concerns above their own. The hun spirits are indeed spirits of kindness and the higher realms of the hun are those of benevolence. It is wonderful to be truly kind. It is a higher grace, and one that is certainly needed. The spirit of benevolence teaches of a kindness that spreads as a strong and generous support. However, to spread this kind of energy, a strong and secure internal core is needed. In much the same way as a beautiful tree can only spread its canopy of leaves, fruits and flowers if the trunk is strong and the roots deep, the spirit of true kindness can only spread if the internal core is strong and powerfully rooted in a sense of who you truly are.

Without this inner strength and power, dissatisfaction and resentment and a kind of lacklustre frustration can emerge. Your power is leached away as your own dreams disappear like scraps of paper in the wind. You find yourself collapsing under the weight of other people's demands, and before you know it, in comes that Dark Dragon once more, cursing and angry. "It's my turn," it roars.

Yes, it has always been your turn. It is the turn of everybody to create their own dream of life.

There is, of course, a balance to be struck between self and others, but the teachings of wood suggest that you include yourself in your own life and in your deeds of kindness, and that through this, you build the growth of your personal power, encouraging the expansion that you need for following your individual destiny.

Your life is intended for you. You are here to discover your personal contribution and to fulfil this calling, however great or small. Seek your own rhythm and your own drumbeat and respond to its cry. The rhythm of life has no time for stagnation but calls in the flows of new and creative energy, which is the substance of health and wellbeing. The hun urge you towards your growth and flourishing, with a sense of energy, and urgency in answering this call. 'The time is now.' In this level of vibration, your own creative rhythm and power does not take from other people or seek to control or manipulate but adds to the kind and creative forces of life. It seeks the fulfilment of all.

Nature is kind in its outpourings. It gives growth to many beings of many different shapes and sizes, and in its spirit of benevolence, there's room for them all to grow. Again, bring to mind a beautiful tree and consider its generosity. The oxygen-producing leaves create the very life-giving breath that we need to exist, and they also produce a canopy of moisture and a refuge against heat from the sun or a dry spot to shelter from the rain. Trees are beautiful, their foliage giving architecture and colour to the landscape. Trees, like other plants, can be farmed and harvested and their wood used for making all manner of things, for building and for warmth. They are a haven for many creatures and home for nesting birds, bugs and insects and other creatures. They provide safety for climbing creatures escaping from less agile predators. The cool of a forest floor provides a welcome haven on a hot and airless summer day. In all these ways and more, trees epitomise the benevolent forces of nature, but their benevolence relies on the strength and power of their healthy growth.

Many people with a spiritual sensitivity recognise that trees, and some more than others, have a 'spirit'. Have you ever relaxed against a strong tree trunk and felt its energy as something other than your own? This energy can emerge as a particular feeling, often of a deep wellbeing. We have a huge and beautiful willow tree in our garden. At times of difficulty or when inspiration refuses to flow, I sit under this tree. I am aware of a strong and deeply magical presence, and often messages arise within me from this presence. It stands like a benevolent guardian right in the centre of our garden and is a haven for many beings, including friends and family who love to sit and absorb its quiet strength.

This tree is huge and in need of pruning. Pruning dead wood and undergrowth facilitates the new and vigorous. Cutting away old growth makes way for the flourishing of the new. The hun urge you towards a precision of focus. What is it in your life that is outworn, cannot flourish and grow any further? Do you keep going over the same thoughts, frustrations, emotions? Do your emotions creep over you like ivy, taking hold and suffocating you? Then please take hold of your sense of power and prune away these old and dead remnants of the past. The past is over but creates good quality experience for the growth of the new. An important task of the spirits of the hun is to bring you into your new and present moment as a gift of consciousness. To be fully awakened is to become more conscious of the shape of your life; the shape of your beliefs, your emotions and your power, your thoughts, your words and your actions.

If you are locked in routine, then you will lose your impetus for imagination and life becomes mundane, empty, 'automatic' and devoid of spirit. You can function perfectly well in automatic, but cannot truly 'live', as the spirit of conscious awareness has disappeared, along with the enlivening power of change, spontaneity and new possibilities. It is time to trim away old routines and old habits and to welcome the spirit of your life back in with wide open arms. Make the decision now to lop away your own dead wood and shed the old leaves of your habits. This alone will create more energy for you to come to life and awaken to opportunities that come your way. To be asleep and lost in routine and habits is to lose focus of the new. Wood qi is about vision, so take away the blind routines and then just look at what happens!

Change the sequence of your day. Change your routines of work, home and leisure. Allow the benevolent East winds of change a little space to blow through you. Be brave and do something that you've always wanted to do but never allowed yourself. The spirits of the hun say, "Yes, you are most definitely allowed." Become active. Move, stretch, flex. Wake yourself up from the worn-out dream of yourself to a conscious awakened dream of how you would like to be.

As much as you are able, stay in the present and see it as the magical gift that it is. The emotions love to go walkabout into the past and love to keep pulling you back there. Keep pruning that old pull of the past away and see it as a powerful resource for your present and the creation of your future. Your past has already shaped you and the gift of experience means that nothing has to be re-enacted or included in your present and your future unless you make the empowered choice to allow it conscious space. Use the power of 'Yes' to bring you back to your present moment and reclaim all that you are, and the power of 'No' to prevent the endless recycling of habits and addictions.

Bring yourself into present time. Habits come from being overly invested in the past, and addictions arise from the frustration of not expressing yourself creatively in your own life. Becoming the author of your life is to write your own story, compose your own symphony, become your own healer, poet and muse. If you could write the story of your life before you were even born, what would you dare to dream and dare to write for yourself?

Meditation for Deep Empowerment

Create Some Space

Sit or lie within your quietness.
Close your eyes and awaken your inner vision.
Ask to be shown the times that you have lost your personal power and the
times that you have slipped and fallen from your path or given your power
away.
Give yourself some time for memories and images to arise from within.
As each one arises, see clearly in what way you disempowered yourself and
claim your energy back from this memory.
Who or what have you given your power away to?
Where are the broken dreams and unrealised dreams? Where is the unfinished
business?
Go through all your memories without blame for anyone else involved, but
simply reclaim that part of yourself that you invested and gave away.
Imagine that you can draw your power back to yourself from all these people
events and fantasies. As your power returns, you may like to use some imagery
such as flowers or crystals coming back to you.
Keep going until you have recovered as much of yourself as you are able to.
Feel kindness towards all the events, people and circumstances who have been
present in your life to teach you about personal power and make a vow not to
become disempowered in your present or in your future.
Create an intention of feeling strongly rooted and
balanced in your own life.

Please repeat this meditation every time you feel disempowered, demotivated, lost, or in some way weakened by events, situations, or by other people.

As you return your lost power to yourself as a gift of soul, begin to plan your strategy towards creating your dreams. How will you achieve what you want to achieve? Think of and include details. Create your map and plan your route, leaving no place for vagueness, but plenty of space for creativity. Your dreams could involve relationships, health, work, home or they could be financially focussed. They could be some of these, all of these, or something entirely different. However, what they all have in common is the strategy needed to set your sights and create a clear and focussed pathway towards bringing your dreams into the sharp focus of reality.

In my experience, I have found that by empowering myself to step out of the stagnation of past emotions and embrace the power of the present and future (please refer to Meditation for Empowerment), I have had more than enough 'zesty' motivation and creative imagination to move with focus and clarity towards my dreams and goals. Exercise, and healthy eating, helps enormously, as does setting myself goals and revelling in the meeting of them.

What would you dare to dream into reality if you knew it
couldn't fail?

It's exciting. Set yourself achievable goals and then raise the bar so that you need to stretch to meet the next ones, as a gift of the wood element is flexibility and extension. Stretching physically, mentally and emotionally expands you and expands the boundaries and structures of your life. Expand into the blueprint of your magical destiny. Make choices of power, whatever they may be. It doesn't matter as long as they mean something to you. You too can become author and magician of your own life transforming the mundane into the magical!

Awakening into
Higher Consciousness

As we rise into the more rarefied vibrational realms, life takes on a new, softer and more magical quality. The whole world appears to arise from an incredible and beautiful divine plan. Without a plan, how could there be any natural balance, and how could the seasons flow one into another? How could the exact conditions arise for life, in its fullest sense, to emerge and to fulfil itself? From this perspective, there is nothing accidental. All life forms have a place in maintaining the integrity and beauty of the divine plan.

With the rising and refining of the qi of the wood element, comes expanded vision. The accompanying awakening brings the realisation of self in relation to life in a larger sense. The soul begins to come to the fore as we become broader, more open in vision, and less inward-looking. Whereas previously, the individual was assertive in the following of a personal dream, ambition or goal, at this level of soul, like the spreading branches of a huge and magnificent tree, the vision sees that as one person fulfils their higher potential, so others can be supported to do the same. Life begins to take the shape of something greater and more inclusive. The story becomes one of 'we' rather than simply 'I', and we can now see with clarity that our own actions and growth affect the whole. At this level, each person takes their place, becoming aware that their individual plans, goals, ideas and dreams are a natural and essential part of the Divinely balanced, greater plan.

The ethereal soul is said to relate to the hun and is sometimes referred to as 'space', or consciousness, as its journey is towards a greater level of awakening or awareness. The growing levels of awareness begins to nudge you, to draw your attention to the quiet whisperings of the soul. It is important to give yourself the space to become aware of what it is that your attention is being drawn towards, as this is the next phase of the unfolding of soul. Perhaps you have overridden, ignored, not given space to these urgings and promptings for some time, and they are becoming difficult to ignore. It may be just the right time to make some adjustments and to pay attention to whatever is being indicated, clearing your inner vision to see what is being presented by your soul.

It may not be a huge task of a massive undertaking, it may be that something, someone, perhaps yourself or a close relationship is longing for a different level of focus. It may be that now is the perfect time for realising that dream that has been in the background for too long. The call of soul is to notice what needs space, attention or focus and to make the necessary moves.

Becoming Benevolence

The hun spirits are spirits of creation whose teaching is of benevolence and kindness. They can help to imbue the imagination with beauty and colourful ideas or prompt your consciousness to notice something that needs attention. They may flow in through dreams awakening the soul to its own longing.

At this level of soul, being kind comes as naturally as the air we breathe. It becomes instinctive, and the ups and downs of life that we used to take so personally, no longer unsettle us to the same extent. There is now a level of space between the self and others, which allows each to follow their own avenues of growth. It becomes natural to be kind; easy benevolence flowing through the soul and into everyday life like warm sunlight. Kindness spreads like a canopy of leaves, guiding the perception to where it is most needed.

Becoming your own magician…
You add your creative spirit to the spirit of creation,
Bringing texture, colour and artistry to your own life,
And giving a touch of magic to life as a whole.

Chapter 3
The Shen Spirits of Fire

Attunement Meditation

The Summer Spirit of Expression

Further down the river ways, the light is brighter, and the waters warm and
flowing.

With the increasing warmth around, you begin to feel an intensity of heat and,
as if in response, the ascending of the pure essence of self as spirit. You rise
soaring as a firebird from the ashes of illusion and delusion, hurt, pain.

As you rise higher, shen spirits flicker like fireflies awakening your heart to the
joy of heavenly callings.

'Yes' is your blissful response.

At last, you are ready to walk your inner fires, ready to burn away the dross and
chaos of what has been. You are AWAKE, and magnificent, your bounded
heart finally free.

'Yes,' you cry again, arms reaching heavenward, to receive gifts of spirit.

This is your moment of exaltation, and that for which you are born.

Shen spirits of heaven flicker again through the contours of your heart, healing
and softening, bringing with them divine gifts of love.

You are love. This is your learning. You are the fires and passions of joy.

Let your fires burn through the darkness of sorrows.

Be sad no more, but open your heart, and then open it

again.

Again.

Again.

Then shine with the pure lights of spirit. Shine your beautiful self out into life, awakening darkened and sorrowful hearts.

Shine the whole of yourself, leaving no part behind.

You are Beautiful.

You are Pure Love.

The Spirit of Summer

The Shen Spirits of the Fire Element

Spirits of Loving Expression

The shen are the spirits of the sun, and summertime, and teach what it is to love from the deepest part of the heart. They are the heavenly messengers whose mission is to carry divine love to human hearts, awakening it to learn the highest ways of love and, through love, transform the energy of grief, sadness or despair into unfettered light. The shen teach of the love that is there for all. It is a love that spreads with the heat and light of a welcoming fire, igniting a spark in all hearts. The heart must be open, peaceful and untroubled to receive these beautiful emissaries of light, whose mission it is to bring a sparkle to even the darkest hours of desolation, encouraging the individual soul to walk the powerful internal fires of awakening and to rise exultant in praise of life as a re-born, re-awakened expression of self.

Can you walk your inner fires?

The Essence of Fire Power

The essence of power of the fire element is to rise to the limits of your personal self, encompassing all that you are with a joyful radiance and as a celebration of being alive! It is to ignite others to do the same by spreading the radiance of your passion for life. Life is exciting and there to be experienced and lived to the limits, and live it, you will!

The Harmonious Resonance of Fire

Season is summer.

Colour is red.

Sound is the joyful laughter of sharing and love.

Aroma is scorched and 'bitter'.

In the body, the Fire element governs the heart and heart protector, the blood and circulation, the body's thermostat and the small intestine.

The qualities invoked by fire are sociability and the warmth of bringing people and circumstances together, joy and happiness, appropriate and loving relationships, creative expression and celebration of life, dynamic activity and loving openness of the heart, which can add a sense of vulnerability.

The Disharmonious Resonance of Fire

Jealousy, possessiveness, vengeance loneliness, closed, overly open, inappropriate or erratic behaviour particularly of a sexual nature, shyness, anxiety, sadness, fluctuations in mood, always seeking the 'Highs' in life, superficiality.

Symptoms – Heart issues, poor circulation, high or low blood pressure, sore throats, inflammatory and painful conditions, insomnia, mania and depression, conditions of stress.

Awakening into Higher Consciousness

Unconditional love and the steady flame of peace that burns gently and brightly no matter what. The living of life is centred within the heart, with the resulting flows of love that reach inwards and outwards as a powerfully healing force of transmutation and joy.

Song of the Fire Element

Fire, magical spirit of life,
The ignitor of
Joy, fun and high voltage energy!
Now here, now gone like sunshine playing with clouds,
It will tease you away from dreary days, from sombre pass times, and bid you
'play with life'.
Play dreamlike in childhood innocence.
Enticing back your laughter,
Your colour,
Your unbridled joy of spirit.
'Sparkle with light',
Call the spirits of Heaven,
'Flow with the colours of your open loving heart.'

Summer

Season of Fire

Yes, it's summer and the fire element is at her fullest and most glorious. Summer is the time of year that the heart yearns for. Light and heat from the sun cheers the spirits, warms the body and opens the senses. Energy is high, plentiful and expressive. The fullness of the sun makes for youthful energy. It's fun. It's playtime. Old and worn routines can now be thrown to the side, making way for something else. New rhythms of longer days and shorter nights are here and there's a definite buzz in the air, an electrifying magic that explodes from the sun at its height in the endlessly blue sky.

Nature is flirtatiously flowing with love, in her beautiful outpourings of outrageous colour – "Look at me, aren't I gorgeous?" In summer, anything goes, flower vying with flower to be the most dazzling, the fullest, the most richly scented, the most beautiful. There's colour everywhere, and down pours the sun, daring nature to keep throwing her blooms up to meet it.

The warmth and light of a high sun in the sky is a strong force of lifting and opening in people and in nature. These strong forces of qi make for rapid and animated activity, as life is suddenly alight with possibilities and the endless expressions in the individual and in the world around.

Summer people live through the forces of their hearts. They are loving, exuberant, and full of enthusiasm, joyful excitement and a contagious warmth. Energy in the forms of ideas, plans and emotions blazes forth in many or all directions at once until, like its element of fire, it becomes diminished if not tempered, contained or positively directed. If not tended and fed with whatever is appropriate to the need in the moment, there's a danger that the flames may dwindle and die back, burning themselves down to cinders and ashes, and like sadness, a veil comes over as the light diminishes. By its very nature, fire has its own volatility that can be tricky to sustain, requiring just the right kind of stimulation and attention. It needs feeding with fuel to keep it active and, like a well-stoked blaze, people with a hot fire element in their makeup really go for the 'highs' in life. They can't be bothered with the mundane, or with things that don't interest them.

Attention is short, and distraction is sought when life becomes drab. 'Life is for fun and play' is their motto. "I want it all!" laughs the fire spirit. This way of being is igniting, contagious and uplifting to those around. When your heart is open, generous and flowing with love, you feel beautiful and energised. You can spread your arms wide and love the whole world!

How the Fire Element
Arises in the Body

In the body, the Fire element governs the heart, the blood and the circulatory system of vessels, veins and arteries. In the digestive system, Fire also governs the metabolic rate and the small intestine. Fire has an affinity with the tongue, giving rise to fast and animated speech and colourful use of body language and expression. A disturbance in fire can also be indicated in speech impediments such as stammering, or loss of vocal power. The fire meridians run up and down the arms, transporting the shen spirits from the heart, through the hands and out towards other people as love and heart-centred healing.

The heart and pericardium meridians arise in and around the heart, flowing down the arms, through the palms of the hands and emerging from the tips of the little finger and the middle finger. The triple heater (responsible for the body's thermostat and circulation) and small intestine meridians begin in the fourth finger and the little finger, respectively, travelling up the arms and the side of the neck, arriving at the side of the head, around the ears and ending in the temples. Unlike the other elements, which have two main meridians, the Fire element has four, indicating the paramount importance of the heart and the spirit of fire.

Fire is easy to invoke and stimulate into a blaze, but difficult to manage, and these four aspects of Fire each have a particular task in its management and organisation. A primary quality of fire is its unpredictability. It can flare and burn with little control or, if not given the right conditions, can smoulder down to ashes and blow itself out. A healthy mind, body and spirit is reliant on the balance, cooperation and maintenance of each aspect of fire. The nature and vital tasks of the pericardium, triple heater and small intestine are to safeguard the wellbeing of the heart, which is the central core of an individual's life. Each of the three has a specific and important role to play as guardian to the health and wellbeing of this vital core.

Fire creates joyful animation and loving warmth and the task of the pericardium is to radiate these qualities both inwards towards the heart and outwards into the body, mind and spirit as a strong and steady rhythm, and to sustain the rhythmic beating of the heart. The heart thrives on love, and love is what it must have. The feelings thrive on love, as do relationships, friendships, and all animate beings. Love is life and the spark of fire that ignites the processes of conception and cell division and which goes on to create a human being. The pericardium is so good at creating love and being love and pouring love.

The triple heater has the task of regulating the inner fires of temperature and the outer fires of emotion. People who are up and down and down and up, happy, sad, laughing and crying all at once, may be displaying an instability in their heating regulator. A steady and constant emotional temperature is what is needed for healthy, constant and well-regulated fire. Chinese medicine divides the body into three burners, or cauldrons. The upper burner is the cauldron of the upper body, with the head, heart and lungs. The middle burner is the cauldron of the middle body, with the organs of digestion, stomach, spleen, liver and gallbladder. The lower burner is the cauldron of the lower body with the organs of elimination, the large intestine, bladder and kidneys. Without a constant level of heat, these processes become slow, sluggish and, with the onset of continual cold, can eventually become compromised and even stop. If the fire burns too strongly for too long, the dangers of overheating can be experienced, with the resultant impact on the health. An obvious manifestation of overheating is overly high blood pressure.

The small intestine has a particular role to play in the safeguarding of the heart. Its task is to receive the contents of the stomach after the initial processes of digestion and to separate what is good and useful from what is bad and of little use. The good is distributed to the body as nourishment, which will ultimately benefit the heart, and the bad is sent down to the organs of elimination to be disposed of. In Chinese medicine, the small intestine is given the name of 'the separator', and it is this task that makes it so invaluable to the health and protection of the heart. If something 'impure' enters the body through food or drink, the health and wellbeing could indeed be compromised. In the same way, if behaviour, emotions or intent are impure or inappropriate, then it is the task of this same process to act as a guide and to steer a person towards a more discerning and appropriate choice. The small intestine then is the spirit of discernment.

The language of the elements is revealed through the complexion, the emotions, the sound of the voice and the aroma that arises around a person. Fire reveals itself as a red or a red and white (English rose) complexion that may be given to flushing or blushing easily. When distressed or depressed, the complexion may drain and begin to show an ashen grey colour. The voice sparkles with laughter, echoing the rising yang energy, which is quick, vibrant.

And alive with movement. The sound is warm and contagious, as though it will break with laughter at any moment. The odour is warm, like hot sunshine, or freshly washed laundry, or bitter and scorched when the fire element is disharmonious. Fiery people make a beeline for the natural 'highs' in life. They are multi-coloured, fast and exciting, resonating with the qi of summer at its height. Fire brings spirit to life and is the most yang aspect of qi – bright, light, open, hot, fast, dynamic. It is the element of joyful personal expression.

How does your spirit of joy openly express itself in your own life?
Give time and space for it to ignite and spread freely through your open and peaceful heart.

The Shen Spirits of Heaven

Can You Rise with Open Heart
To Your Fullest Expression?

Fire sparkles with vibrant light and teaches of the innocent delights to be experienced in just playing, laughing and enjoying life to the full. Fire teaches of the joy of open and expansive expression of self. How to add your own vibrant colours to the world?

Fire spirits usher in the phase of full creative maturity, of full realisation of self as an enlightened being of love. Fire is fast moving, transformative and passionate. Its nature is to change, to transmute and ultimately transcend the mundane. Its calling is to connect with the authentic self in the higher heavenly fields of love and bliss. Bring to mind an image of tongues of fire reaching to their full height, crackling, impressive and rising like a bird, exalted and beautiful. The firebird urges expansion into the fullest expression of spirit, encouraging you to spread your own wings and to reach for the pure spirit of who you can ultimately as pure being of love and light.

The spirits of the heart are called the shen, and their mission is to come and go as flickering messengers, flying birdlike back and forth between heaven and people. They are the joyful emissaries of light whose task is to carry love, peace and bliss to be received by generous open hearts. They are warm, bright and joyful, happily making their roosting place in empty and peaceful hearts, where they can not only rest and take sanctuary but also impart their precious messages into a pure and open-heart space.

Disturbances and volatile emotions create agitation, igniting their flighty nature and sending them skyward once more in search of serenity. Their flickering nature is like firelight and can be seen in the sparkle behind clear bright eyes, in the sheen of healthy skin and can be heard in the happy sound of laughing. The shen spirits ignite the spirit of an individual life, giving it colour and energy. They visit during sleep and meditation, when all is quiet and still, settling in the temple of the peaceful and serene heart, where they can impart their heavenly gifts of vitality, zest and radiance.

The shen circulate through the bloodstream, igniting qualities of warmth and vivacity throughout mind and spirit as well as through the entire body. Chinese mythology tells us that the spirit rides upon the blood as a rider upon a horse, directing and controlling the speed and the flows of blood and qi. The shen flow outwards, bringing a healthy and lively animation to relationships, interactions and to life itself. They bring ideas and creativity, inspiration and the impulse for expression and vitality.

If you have a strong affinity to fire (or strong shen), you are the 'life and soul of the party', lighting and igniting the atmosphere wherever you go. Your natural warmth draws people to you as you beam your sunlight outwards with an open generosity of spirit. You are sociable and fun loving, impulsive and spontaneous. Your special gift is to draw the sparkling fire forwards in people, events and situations, giving lightness of spirit and the power of transformation. 'Why be sad, when you can be happy?' is your message.

However, fire has an innate vulnerability, and can change in an instant, being dependent on external conditions such as fuel and weather conditions. We all have experience of a fire that dies down and blows itself out if left unattended. When fire burns to ashes, it becomes cold and lifeless, and this quality can be experienced in people who have a particular sadness or depth of depression that is utterly devoid of life. In acupuncture terms, this is called 'lack of fire', and feels so sad, it is completely desolate.

Imagine a landscape, cold, grey, dark and barren of colour, its people isolated and struggling, depressed and anxious. What vegetation and crops that can be grown emerge as lifeless and stunted; day and night appear the same – grey and unchanging. How to survive? How to go on? All is quiet, drab, desolate. One day, as if from nowhere, a mighty light ascends in the grey dreary sky. It rises in its magnificence as a fiery orb. Its majesty has the presence of a god, tossing out peaches, golds and pinks across the dank sky. As it rises further, as if by magic, our previously grey and dreary landscape is graciously transformed. The effects are intense and immediate, as land and people are flooded with joyful life-giving vitality. Faces lift in laughter and vegetation is filled with life-giving vigour. All is beautiful and teeming with life, people and nature, happy and well.

Imagine too, if this force was permanent, daylight perpetual and heat unbroken. Imagine the effects on our landscape, as it scorches beneath what is now perceived as a torturous and relentless heat. The land is now burnt and infertile, its people hot, angry and warring for what little produce is available. The heat goes on and on.

Life as we know it cannot tolerate or sustain itself in the extremes. Too much heat or too little heat are both harmful. So too in people; too much fire can overheat the body and the emotions, which can arise as painful and inflammatory conditions and an inflammatory temperament. In the same way, too little fire is detrimental, creating cold and aching conditions and a lacklustre temperament.

A gift of fire, then, is its expression of impermanence. Now you see it and now you don't. It is teasing in its changeable nature. It rises and then is gone again. It emerges and then dies back down. Fire, like laughter, reaches its height and then dies away. It is as sunlight coming and going as clouds pass over the sky.

Fire is a teacher of the nature of what is appropriate, and what is not. If fire burns too brightly, it will scorch and may devour all in its pathway with a lack of care that potentially causes devastation. If it does not burn brightly enough, like a damp squib, it will splutter and fail. Learn to attune with your own heart, feeling its resonance and its rhythm. Begin to listen within to understand your own spirit of fire.

Feel into Your Loving Heart

Place your open left hand in the centre of your chest
Take a huge deep breath from your abdomen right up into your chest. Hold for
a moment.
Gently release.

Listen to the beating of your heart.

Feel the rhythm of life beating its pulsation of love throughout your body.

Your heart creates its own natural rhythm answering the call to open and expand into ever more loving flows of light.

Be with the peace of your own natural rhythm.

Ask yourself –

How does fire arise within me?

Does it rage or glow gently?

Is it easily ignited?

Is it harmful or life-giving?

Does it bring me happiness?

Do I know the feelings of bliss?

Hold yourself gently and peacefully within your own space and give yourself these words.

'Peace reigns within the contours of my heart.

I am in perfect balance.

My way is the path of love, and it is through love that my spirit transforms my life and soars to ever greater horizons.

I am love.

And I give thanks for the love that flows within and without, having honour for my own emerging spirit.'

Joy – Emotion of Fire

The Exultant Gift of Spirit

Just as summer weather conditions can vary, so can the fire spirit fluctuate through a huge range of emotions from the highest to the lowest. Just as flames can surge to the heights, so they can quickly burn down to ashes. Much as clouds can move across the bluest and clearest sky bringing rain, so emotions can cloud a sunny landscape, bringing tears and sadness. Fiery people can go from high to low in an instant, having the capacity for an expansive range of feelings and emotion. Being open-hearted and easily moved, there is a natural resonance and response to other people's feelings, to sadness and to joy.

With the rising and expansion of qi, like butterflies the emotions seek the light, and the element of fire loves nothing more than to become ignited and fully charged by life's excitements and passions. Crackling and dancing with feelings, emotion and passion, high and colourful is the nature of rising fire, and emotions are reflected in movement and speech. Often audacious, often inappropriate, but always expressed. Strong passions create the excitement of heat but can't be sustained for long, going from high to low in the blink of an eye. Fiery people can be extroverted and passionate, demanding attention and high levels of entertainment as fuel to fan the flames.

Joy is the natural expression of fire. Wild and abandoned joy is exhilarating, but as a default setting can put excessive demands upon the mind, body and spirit, and can emerge as a demand from life to 'make me happy!' Loving to be at the heart of things, fiery people will stop at nothing to catch the attention, however inappropriate.

Rising fire is illuminating, exciting, unpredictable and dangerous. In contrast, it can be warming and gentle, burning with a predictability and constancy, and it shows its many faces throughout our lives: fast, vulnerable, volatile, changeable unpredictable, loving, open-hearted.

A single match can start a forest fire, which if unchecked can cause untold damage. In the same way, a single thoughtless word or action can set off an unpredictable and potentially hazardous emotional state. Fire can be doused by the waters of reason or it can be fed by the dry wood of anger and fanned by winds of self-righteousness.

Fire likes an audience. The fiery soul loves nothing more than a public display, expecting those around to rise to similar heights, becoming hurt by refusals to participate, but taking solace in the entertainment they have provided. Fire is the joker, the 'life and soul', the 'anything for a laugh' character.

They will become outrageous, flirtatious, hilarious, whether or not the situation demands it. When all eyes are on them, they can settle into the hot spot at the centre (the heart), where the attention fans their flames of emotional need, which craves compliments and admiration. As it is fed, so it can give its natural love and warmth of spirit. Fire loves to include everyone in the 'party' of life. When the passion of fire has consumed everything in its path and given all it can of itself, it finally dies down, temporarily satiated.

However, the fire element also has a softer side, which may be found hiding under a gentle veil of shyness, and a dislike of public display and too much attention. Being sometimes overly concerned with the feelings of other people, this aspect of fire can retreat into the shade. It seems that everyone else is partying and leading the 'high life', and this gentle soul can feel forgotten, excluded and 'left out in the cold'.

Fire can be as steady and gentle as a candle flame, or the warm fire that burns in the hearth as a welcome home. However, beware, fiery people can be changeable and unpredictable, one moment shining like the sun in a cloudless sky, and the next taken over by a thunderstorm. Like butterflies, they are infinitely colourful and love nothing better than to dance, flit and flutter with flows of energy. Their inconsistency urges them to them dart from one thing to the next and the next, having fun and creating joy, but not looking back at the potential havoc they may have caused. 'Live for the moment' is their motto, sometimes leaving a trail of unfinished projects, ideas, relationships, as the new and exciting is often pursued.

Being very sociable, they often have a wide circle of friends and social acquaintances because their greatest dread is to be on their own or forgotten. Generous and attractive, fire people will shower you with attention. They will fall in love with you and that love will endure, making you feel like a king or queen until the next distraction, diversion or more interesting 'catch' comes into view. Fast moving and inconstant, their desire is to devour as many of life's riches and experiences as they can, and they will use these to fan their own flames of growth and expansion.

However, high and hot emotions can burn out, turning to the ashes of exhaustion, and the constant joking and humour can often hide a soft and tender heart. It can be a social mask designed to keep people at arm's length as a protection from hurt but is also a call from the heart to be truly loved. On the other side of this emotional spectrum is the sadness so often felt as the joy dies away. This level of sadness is profound, being the polar opposite to the heady heights of joy. It can encompass feelings of isolation as 'all the world seems to be having fun except me'. All this emotion takes its toll and can be tiring for the heart. Better to keep a gentle fire constantly burning than to have occasional crazy firecrackers, which not only burn themselves out, but also might inadvertently jump up and scorch someone, whether you, or someone else.

People who resonate with the softer side of the fire element can be tentative, gentle, shy and vulnerable, their fire is softer and more enduring, like a warming and welcoming fire on a cold night. These people are like the gentler blooms, one minute reaching for the sun, and the next falling back into the shade through lack of confidence, or through the unwillingness to tolerate the unyielding glare. Rather than reaching outwards in extroverted exuberance, they may reach inwards towards their inner sun, seeking the deeper and more hidden sides of life. These people will not take life so lightly, but can be the seekers and searchers, needing the companionship of others who seek the same path of the spirit.

The heart meridian emerges into the mouth and travels down the tongue, suggesting that speech arises from the feelings in the heart, and that words spoken will have an impact on one's own heart and the hearts of others. Gentle and loving heart qi will give rise to gentle and loving speech, whilst the agitated and raging heart will give rise to agitated and raging words spoken in the heat of the moment. Tempers can be intense, short-lived, burning themselves out quickly, or they may smoulder incessantly like hot coals. Usually very open, very vocal, nothing remains hidden for long as the urge to share overrides the wisdom of silence. Stuttering or loss of speech can indicate a disharmony in the fire element, often brought about through distress or trauma, and either peaceful silence or the expression of a loving heart, may be what is needed to restore harmony.

Contemplation to Invoke Healthy Fire Energy

This contemplation will help you to release the internal noise excessive emotions create and to find a sense of equilibrium as a place of peace and restoration for the heart.

Sit quietly…

Breathe softly allowing your heartbeat to settle into its own steady rhythm.
Gently focus your attention within the centre of your chest.
Imagine a beautiful golden sphere of light hovering over and within this area and encompassing your heart.
In your imagination, start to find your way to the centre of this sphere, gently moving through the colours and contours of your heart space.
Give all your hurt, your emotional pain and heartbreak to the golden light.
Keep giving it and pouring it out of your deepest and most hidden places.
The light will draw it from you, transforming it through the grace of love.
Keep sinking towards the centre, until you arrive at a place of great beauty, gentleness and peace.
Here you come to rest within a place of deep peace and softness.
Like a haven it draws itself around you.
Here you are safe and protected.
Here you are radiant with the spirit of love.
Allow the radiance to flow through every part of your body and then outwards into your life.

When you are ready, gently return to your present moment, giving yourself a little time to adjust to the changes happening within yourself.
This energy is deeply healing, calming pain and trauma and transforming difficulties with its light and loving radiance.
From this place, life can become transformed, disharmonies falling away as burdens of the past, leaving the present joyful, renewed and undisturbed.

Fire Element as Love

"It's all about love," sing the crackling flames, and the spirits of fire make love above all else their life story and their goal. Those with powerful and transmuting fire as their key resonance are deeply healing. They may or may not be healthcare professionals, healers or therapists, but their presence has an electrifying radiance that transforms denser and heavier energies, being warming and restoring. This inherent radiance and warmth can make them very powerful leaders, having the natural capacity for public display and the ability to ignite others and to encourage them to give of their creative best. If not leaders of others, the natural love of life kindles their creative capability to rise to the top of their own field and become successful within their own domain.

They are the natural comedians, entertainers and jokers amongst us, or conversely the gentle shiners of light. Light comes from the sun and these people are the gentle flames that lovingly light the way, having a natural capacity to 'see the light' in a given situation. As a light shines into a darkened room illuminating even the dank and dusty corners, so the light of spirit can shine through dusty or forgotten areas of people or of life in a greater context, bringing the illumination of 'enlightenment'.

The Fire Element out of Balance

When the Spirit Becomes Disturbed

A disturbed, closed or angry nature may frighten away the gentle shen spirits, who are drawn to earth through loving peaceful hearts. In Chinese mythology, the shen are depicted as a flock of pure white birds, coming and going from heaven to earth. They alight during restful sleep when all is peaceful, bringing messages of grace from heaven. The shen are not only the spirits of fire but are also the spirits of life itself.

A strong and constant fire gives strong and constant growth. Constancy is a keynote of a healthy heart, helping it to avoid the extremities of highs and lows which can create strain upon the yielding heart. Constancy of being creates constancy in love, enabling it to move and to flow in an expanded, unconditional state beyond the everyday emotional turbulence.

Ancient Chinese masters saw the heart as a loving and peaceful emperor and the protective sheath as a beautiful palace and garden. When the emperor is peaceful, well-guarded and joyful, he can rule in a loving and harmonious way, spreading peaceful order and wellbeing throughout the kingdom. The reign will be a gentle and magnanimous one, with all processes functioning happily according to their true place and true nature. A happy and relaxed heart is a happy and relaxed mind, body and spirit, peaceful and secure, free from stresses and disruptive emotions. Now higher flows of love can spread as fire throughout the body, mind, spirit and beyond into life, as healing and goodwill.

There is a state of imbalance in Chinese medicine known as shen disturbance. If the sovereign, or emperor no longer has charge over his peaceful domain, aspects of the mind, body, emotions and spirit can fall into the realms of chaos and crisis. When the shen are disturbed, often as the result of severe or repeated shock or trauma, the whole self becomes chaotic as the all-important connection with heaven becomes distorted, compromised or even broken.

Shen disturbance leads to extreme feelings of restless anxiety, a general disturbance of the spirit, and emotional and mental disorders and symptoms. People with this level of imbalance may become nervous and overly anxious about even the smallest things, feeling unsettled and unable to rest, relax or sleep. They may jump from one thing to another as the attention flickers like flames fanned by a breeze. The energies of imbalance flash and spark, from one emotional crisis to the next, from one idea to the next, from one resolution to the next in a constant whirl of confusion. Dreams may be unsettled or frightening, and you may feel as though the light has gone out of your life.

People with imbalance in their fire element may be unpredictable. Relationships become volatile and unstable, often through the propensity towards aggression or at the other end of the spectrum, the propensity towards severe anxiety and depression, which can, in extremes, be suicidal in nature. Symptoms can be 'hot', sharp and stabbing painful symptoms, or 'angry' conditions such as eczema or acne. Blood pressure and pulse may be high, and the body may sweat profusely. The heart can display symptoms such as irregular heartbeat, palpitations, or more serious cardiovascular conditions.

Symptoms of 'lack of fire' will be cold in nature and slow. The blood pressure may be low, the hands and feet always cold, and painful conditions may be aching and dragging in nature. The heart has no desire for excessive highs and lows, but longs for nothing more than natural and peaceful equilibrium. Emotional excess in all its colours takes a toll on the heart, whether excessive ecstasy, rage, sadness, it proves too much for the heart which loves the balance and equilibrium of a steady flame of joy. Highly charged emotional states can cause disruption to the shen spirits of heaven, and a gentle constancy is just what they need to encourage them to stay and dispense their gifts from the heavenly planes.

Love Affirmation

My heart is gentle and peaceful.
I attract loving people and am alight with joy.
I am deeply and graciously in love with
my own life…

The Pink Flame

The flame is a symbol, which expresses the season of summer perfectly.
Fire purifies, removing all in its path. A very powerful and destructive force
when untamed or out of control, but also very fast and effective at clearing
what is no longer needed.
Light a candle and sit before it, encouraging your body and your mind to gently
relax and become soft and receptive.
Breathe deeply and evenly as the gentle candlelight holds you in its glow.
Visualise a gentle pink flame growing up around you and coming from deep
within the earth.
Let it gently consume you, rising above your head.
Feel the constancy and warmth working its way through all parts of your body.
Relax and allow this flame to move through any pain, difficulty or constriction.
Imagine that it has the power to calm, and to take away all your agitation,
anxiety, your hurt and your suffering.
The flame gently flickers around you and within you, shimmering light burning
through the heavy burdens of anxious and worried thoughts.
Let it find its way, flickering as a light in the darkness.
As the flame subsides, or just blows itself out, it takes with it all negative
emotions, fears and unwelcome thoughts. It leaves you glowing with light,
calm and clear.
Your beautiful heart is calm and clear and flowing with healing love.

Moving into the Shadowlands of the Fire Element

Venturing into the Hidden Depths to Reclaim Your Loving Self

In the shadowlands, lurk the lower realms of the heart. People with fire as their archetype are open-hearted, their imbalances arising from emotional hurt or injury. They are often termed 'too open' or 'too trusting' and because of their openness can fly off like butterflies unprotected and vulnerable towards the next possibility, the next relationship, the next party, always searching for the fun, for something else, for more love, more affection, more passion, more extremes, more excitement, but ultimately the deeper search is for love.

Beware the sting as the gentle butterfly turns into its fierier counterpart. Wasps and bees are fire beings and can give a nasty puncture if provoked. So too can a fiery person. Be careful how you approach, you may get stung or burnt if you venture too close at the wrong moment. Timing is all important. Deep in the lands of the hidden shadowy self, hides the hurt and the pain which is often well camouflaged by a sting in the tail, fiery laughter and fun. In contrast, the shadow can show itself through a sadness so deep that it is tangible to those around. It feels as though the sun has fallen from the sky, leaving the world of this person in gloom and darkness. The spark has gone from the eyes and life has become so hard and lacklustre.

In these shadows, dwell the hurts and heartaches, the envy, jealousy, resentment and hatred. The mourning for love and a longing to love and to be loved in return dwell in this difficult and dark place. These feelings and emotional states all arise out of the lower darkened and scorched fires - burning wounds, emotional pain, unrequited love and the pain of loss. The tender folds of the heart begin to shut down, preserving itself from further hurt, damage and betrayal.

As the heart shuts down, the outer layers can become defensive and can harden in an attempt to stave off encounters and emotions that it considers dangerous. If this continues for too long, then the inner folds of the heart can also become affected, beginning to harden and close, and this heart, over time, becomes deadened and dark and cruel.

Here is seen the mirror of the Fire element rising from the shadows and reflecting its own hurt in the hurting of others. "This is how I feel, and I want you to feel this way too," is the cry of the untransmuted Fire. It arises scorching and dangerous as a dragon, the fires of raw emotion blazing from its mouth. The screech of the fire dragon cries, "I am burnt and wounded, so I will burn you in return." It both creates shock and arises from shock or trauma, when the heart that wanted to flow with its birthright of love became damaged and wounded, blackened with smoke. This illustrates an extreme, the dragon being isolated and separated feeling damaged and disillusioned with a life of harshness and bitterness.

In contrast, a person may fling themselves out into life, being desperately inappropriate, often sexually, attracting encounters and relationships that perpetuate the damage. Sexuality can be wielded like a weapon of fire, hot and deadly.

The soul is really shouting out, trying to attract the attention of the conscious mind to heal the hurt! It creates patterns and continuums of events and relationships to draw attention to what needs to be healed and addressed. "Please stop the pain and the burning." This way can go on and on until the person becomes ready to encounter the dragon, and the deeper needs of the heart, being prepared to heal and transform the damage. As healing progresses, there may be a readiness to encounter the fire initiation of healing and alchemy that transforms the dull lead of mundane and lowly emotions into the golden gifts of spirit.

Fire on the Rise

Freeing Yourself from Patterns of Pain

We are creatures of habit, and perpetuate and recreate the same patterns again and again, until the 'aha' moment of 'If I want something different to happen in my life, I have to change,' or 'If I want love, then I must become loving.' The change must come from within before it is reflected on the outside in intimate friendships and relationships. The mirror of Fire says that 'We must love ourselves before we are ready for another to love us.'

Fire, when burning too rapidly or too brightly, can damage the gentle contours of the heart. When out of balance, the energy of excess fire wants to possess the focus of their desire, setting up a firewall of rage and jealousy if their position is threatened. The fires of jealousy can be all consuming, and lead to extreme agitation and unrest. There is no peace, and the purity of love is consumed in jealous fires of envy and revenge.

On a softer note, jealousy emerges from hurt and wounded love. Knife wounds of betrayal and unrequited love can go very deeply, sometimes to the level of soul, and can take much time, care and love to heal. Sometimes the hurt is experienced throughout life in different ways, as the continuum of this deep wound offers itself up to the conscious mind for healing. If your relationships keep ending in the flames of despair, take some time to look further back for the original cause.

The Fire Spirits of Love Ask;

'Are you ready to release more fully and to become love?
Are you ready to radiantly love through all your pain as a gentle and potent
force of spirit power?'

Healing the Pain of Hurt

Take several gentle breaths.
Settle your attention in the centre of your chest, the realm of your spiritual heart.
If you have been hurt, you may feel fragile and emotional as you settle in this space.
Gently breathe through these feelings.
Take your time. Be gentle and loving as you enter this sacred inner space.
Breath by peaceful breath, sink more deeply towards the centre of your heart.
You may feel hurt and emotion arising. Take very gentle steps and calming breaths, acknowledging the feelings as they arise, without judgement. These emotions, memories and images are stored within the realms of your heart space and need to be addressed with care and with gentle honour.
When you feel ready, ask for an image of the origin of your pain.
You may receive several images and memories, but gently keep going back and back until you stop.
Observe with your inner eye as though you are watching for a scene to unfold.
What's happening?
How do you feel?
Be very gentle with yourself.
When you come back to the present moment, take some time to write as much as you can about what you saw or what you felt before it fades like a dream.

If repeated over time, this healing meditation can be very helpful. You may like a close friend to be with you if your pain is too overwhelming. Ask your friend to help you to unravel thoughts, feelings and images and to hold you in a loving and steady energy as you go through this healing journey. Please don't worry if it's too much to handle, just gently approach this space within and then gently leave again. It will become easier over time. Call on spiritual help, perhaps your guardian angel or a higher divine being. You will feel safe and held. Please never go further or deeper than you can cope with, and if it seems too much, please ask for professional help from an accredited practitioner.

The power of the shen spirits is the power of peaceful and unconditional love. Their task is to usher the graces of the heavenly planes down into the heart, enabling this graciousness to be expressed outwardly and expansively on earth from one heart to another, bringing love and light into everyday life. With the shen, life becomes a celebration of the joy of life from an internal sense of peaceful love. This way of being transforms the mundane into the magical, turning the most ordinary into the extraordinary, and is the gift of transformation offered by the shen. Natural vitality rises, and the capacity for love increases, bringing effortless healing through all levels of being. Love and laughter are contagious, spreading like wildfire from person to person and from heart to heart.

Fire teaches of the joy of personal expression and the healing resonance of pure and unconditional love. It is the rising of the sun in our lives, urging us to expand to new heights in celebration of the very essence of life itself. The warmth of the sun brings natural laughter and communion of spirit, creating a softer resonance. The shen spirits teach playfulness and urge us not to take ourselves and our own life too seriously. "Look outwards and upwards," they encourage and prompt us towards humour and a lightness of heart, urging us to dance brightly with the flows of life. With this lightness of heart and spirit, comes a spontaneous outpouring of the rich substance of love.

As the emotions of fire become lighter and more consistent, deeper openings of the heart take place and hidden feelings of loving peace emerge as a more reliable and profound way of being. It is from this space that love and joy blend and then emerge as a strong and healing flame of light.

Live lightly
Live brightly
Live peacefully

In summer, life reaches its fullest expression of colour and beauty. This resonance is echoed in the call of the shen to bring each of us to our fullest colour and the open expression of our individual gifts of spirit. The call is to expand and to reach higher until we can expand no more. This is the fulfilment of our most dynamic heavenly aspect. The energy of summer is naturally vibrant and uplifting, creating the ideal opportunities for the spirit power of growth.

Live openly
Live expansively
Live your gifts

There is an acupuncture point called Palace of Weariness. This point is a place of safety and refuge for the exhausted patient, whether weary from overwork or from deep emotional hurt. Find this point in the centre of the palm and just a little towards the little finger. As you massage it, bring to mind the love and wisdom of your family and your ancestors. Feel a part of the spirit of the great lineage and bloodline that has brought you to this life. Rest and take refuge in this haven of peaceful love and allow your heart to open to receive the purity of love that it needs to be healthy and at ease with itself.

Here be restored,
and
Here be opened to receive the gifts of heaven
Lie your head on silken cushions,
Feeling the gentle summer breezes
From gardens far below.
Closing tired eyes,
Resting heavy limbs.
Sleeping dreamless sleep

Rising Higher

The Wounded Healer as Archetype

How Is the Spirit of Your Life?

Are you fulfilled in the expression of your spirited and passionate self?

What do you love?

We are here to learn to love through the teachings of the heart. To love self, to love others, to love the spirits of life itself. The shen teach of excitement and adventure, and when life is imbued with these spirited gifts, it takes on a different feel. A life lived without love is a life devoid of spirit. Love makes a potent contribution, it ignites possibility and colour, magically transforming the drabbest and most colourless. All contributions made through love are deeply healing, and your own gifted contribution will be under the direction of your soul. The ways of spirit urge you to express yourself to the highest extent and to experience this expression as the joy of life itself.

If soul is the individual,
then spirit is the igniting force.
Whatever you want,
whoever you are
and
wherever you go,
blaze a loving trail to
spirit power your life.

Your way may be to inspire other people, or just to make people laugh and smile. A quiet act of loving kindness can lighten the heart and work like sparkling drops of magic. Learn to love people in their own language. What would they respond to? What is their way? To miss another's language is to miss the opportunity to deepen your communication, and what you give may be missed.

Your own way may be to leap outrageously and daringly into life, creating rainbow magic of colourful experience. You may be shy and quiet or bold and confident, but you can love! We can all answer the message of the shen spirits, which is to love, love and love. Love who you are and love what you do. Learn to love yourself if it does not come naturally. Falling in love with your own life can ignite a once ordinary life into an extraordinary quest of spirit. Dare yourself to be brighter, higher, more loving!

As you love, your energy will take on a new and lighter resonance, helping the spirits of shen to fulfil their mission as emissaries of heavenly bliss. The path of healing is the path of love. Love can move mountains and change the world, spreading its warmth and igniting hearts. The power of love is deep, wide and hugely transformative and has the power to change everything.

As love flows and the light of spirit ignites the soul, the calling of the divine is heard. What is your calling of spirit? Many people I know who have answered a call to healing embody the archetype of the Wounded Healer. The wounded healer can heal through the infinite compassionate love gained through experiencing such intense life-changing pain that higher levels of the heart are awakened.

These wounds arise through trauma. They are of a potentially life-threatening, and most certainly life-changing, in nature. They can come from physical or emotional pain and sear their burning way through the realm of the heart, deeply into the soul. They can reach to the very essence of a person and have the capacity to change them forever. The fires that burn from deep within burn away the old and outworn self, the emotions and lower thoughts of a darkened nature. Cries arise from the soul for its release from the lower emotional spheres of suffering, from the release of feelings such as bitterness, hatred, resentment, jealousy and anger, all of which arise from the denser nature of a closed heart.

This can prove to be a pivotal time of choice. Which path to choose? The path of glowering resentment for the painful blows from life, or the path of rising to higher spheres through the powerful transformation of love?

The pain from these wounds cannot be assuaged by emotional outpourings as these only amplify its dread depths. It is time for you to walk your inner fires, and this is deeply personal and has the flavour of an initiation. The soul is ready for the embrace of something different, something better, something higher. It is ready to enter the higher domains of love. This phase of spiritual growth takes you on a rite of passage from the gross, mundane everyday life through to the brighter, finer and more rarefied spheres of light and is divinely led and divinely inspired.

It has the Source of all, as the strong guiding force, changing and transforming the very contours of the self that you used to know. The Source bids you, "Be strong enough to heal yourself." There is no other way.

Heal Myself...?

I am looking for you, oh Source of my being.
I am ready for you, God,
Or am I...?
Will you ask of me again, what I cannot do?
Always I search for you, always looking.
I see you in the shaft of light casting jewels across the still lake
I see you in the sunlight breaking through the endless rising river mist
You are there in the twinkling of an eye,
In the laughter pealing from a child.
The fun, the dazzling times...
And now, there are you, God, my soul torn and tattered.
My soul which is yours, which I have returned to you again and again in loving devotion.
You bid me, "Heal myself..."
You bid me, "Rise from the wreckage..."
You bid me, "Become the qualities you most need..."
You call me on to holy ground to become whole myself once more,

freeing my Soul from the savage grip of slavery and devotion to suffering,
and offering it new and deeper horizons of
love.
Heal myself… and the journey begins…

You feel isolated and alone, having fallen so deeply into the abyss. The call is to overcome the darkness of the heavy earthbound emotions of personal love, and to embrace the higher, deeper, wider less personal love. The new way is towards something greater, releasing the self-pity of personal pain and broadening, widening and breaking old bonds. Yours is the pain suffered by many, and your healing will become the healing of many as you rise beyond its constrictions. This wound becomes the portal away from the isolated lower self into the higher realms of the ensouled self. It is the battleground between higher and lower, good and bad, light and dark, angel and demon, heaven and hell. The battle about which many myths and stories have been written is played out within the contours of yourself, your own heart, and is reflected and made visible in the world at large. When these internal battles are resolved, deep healing and change takes place.

Some traditions liken this awakening of the self to a great and magnificent bird awakening to open its wings and to soar into the higher contours of life. Many have heard of the phoenix, a mythological bird who burns away to ashes at the end of its life. Legend tells us that the fledgling phoenix arises to new life from the ashes of the parent bird. The fires of the higher self burn away the outworn lower self, and a new being of spirit emerges.

The gift of the fire element is to burn and transform, clearing the way for the growth of the new.

When I found myself walking my own inner fires, I knew that what I was experiencing was no ordinary pain or difficulty. Never before had I experienced such trauma. No usual help or techniques were of very much use. I was on my own and it felt like a fight to the death. Indeed, it was. Although I was able to work and to function in the outside world, there was something so deep and so potent at work inside me that was far beyond my everyday control.

Eventually, I felt something emerging that I had not felt before. I experienced both a rising and a death, as here I was face to face with my own self and my own choices. The choices were stark and simple. What to hold on to and allow to live inside me, and what to allow to die? What qualities to invoke and what to let go of? With the wild passion for life itself and through the power of my love for my husband and my children, something began to take shape inside me, and slowly, infinitely slowly I began to re-birth myself and to rise, phoenix-like from the death and ashes of my old and discarded self.

Never again would I be the same. Never again would I feel or react in the same way. I felt so strong and so honed by the fires of all that I had been. I felt re-shaped, transmuted, stronger, lighter, reborn and was able to hold myself steadily enough for powerful flows of love to pour freely through the wounded gash in my heart.

When viewed through this wound, life appears different. The sharp and incisive knife of pain has opened the heart and has created a gateway to something different. My own heart, in my mind's eye, took on the appearance of an orb of silver light, which looked to me like a great moon or an opalescent pearl. It was emerging from an open gash in my chest, and when I first saw it during a moment of quiet reflection, I knew that it was part of my new birthing. The gash was, of course, spiritual and not physical.

I had been forged by the deep the fires of my soul and had survived, exalted but, at the same time, deeply humbled. I don't say this from any sense of ego because what happened was almost entirely behind the scenes, beyond my awareness. Perhaps what I experienced was what in some traditions could be called the death of the ego.

As I entered the fires, the only thing left for me was to hold tightly on to my deep sense of faith that something infinitely bigger, broader, more compassionate and wiser was in charge. I am now in the hands of my soul and answerable to the divine.

A Blessing

May the fires of love light your way through the deep abyss of your darkness.
May they be gentle and kind, bright and strong,
Transforming the old and outworn into the bliss of pure love.
May you be joyful, exalted, radiant and vital.
And
May you share the love of the mighty spirit and be loved mightily in return.

Awakening into the Level of Soul
(Higher Consciousness)

Get excited!
Don't be afraid to let yourself go to where the fires of love take you.
Love with all your heart and flow this spirit power throughout your life.
Ignite yourself and blaze with glorious beauty and the courage to be you.
As a loving spark of the eternal, give yourself fuel, energy, movement to take
on the world.
Be dazzling and contagious in your light.
Then flow all of this into the world and beyond.
Give thanks.
Love is the force that awakens, enlivens and generates the miraculous. What
miracles would you like to experience?
Be that love, and be those miracles, and then watch the miraculous unfolding
within and around you.

Love is pure magic and is the incredible bond that holds us together through all
of life and then through death.
And beyond into the mystery.

Life is full of mystery, and the shen spirits bring the light of awakening into
the dark of unknowing. Becoming a conscious part of this mystery, adds your
light to the greater light and your enthusiasm for learning and discovery to the
great wealth of knowledge. Within the arena which is generated by the light of
love as a potency and power, all becomes known and all revealed, to be
acknowledged, learnt from and transformed where necessary. In the light,
everything is uncovered, presenting the opportunity for greater awakening and
expansion into the alignment with your soul.

The overriding spirit of your own life is also called the spirit of shen and is to be found in the alignment of your soul with the choices you make and your path in life. The shen ask, "How well is your life unfolding for you? Do you feel at peace with your own self, with your own ways and with your own unfoldment?"

Take the time needed to draw back when prompted to do so, because it is within the constancy of a peaceful heart, gentle and still, where the deeper answers that you seek may come to you. The peaceful and constant heart will prompt you to follow your own spirit and to recognise the guidance that is offered.

Visualise your internal fires softening down to a constant flickering glow like a candle flame. A fire cannot always blaze to its full height, for that would be too extreme to sustain, but it must draw back, perhaps even to glowing coals or a gentle flame, as though taking a breath, only to rise once more when time and conditions are right.

Love is deep healing and deep spirit power. Become very good at loving and let love bypass all matters of the mind. To live within the realms of the heart is to enter into the Initiation of Fire. Learn first to love yourself, selflessly, constantly and peacefully. Be responsive to your own fluctuations and changes, always ready to witness difficulties and transform them with the light power of pure love. Over time, this will spread its transformative warmth, out towards friends, family, those close to you, and then out into the wider world with its gaping need for love. You as spirit power can take your place in igniting even the darkest and most closed hearts and minds, as you put aside limitations and become a pure flame of love.

A Meditation Prayer for Deep Forgiveness

I call upon you, Great Spirit of Love,
Source of Life,

God,

Goddess...

You who teaches me to love, please teach me to forgive.

Bless me with the knowing, that as I release and finally let go, then those whom I have been holding will also be released and will also be able to let go.

I ask that we become free and unbounded.

And

Through this release, may I become more aligned with the deepening of my

soul,

and

with You

as I

Journey towards the divine light of healing.

In this level of high resonance, it become easier to forgive past hurts, wounds, unkind words... as true and deep forgiveness forges great paths into the highest realms that we as spirit humans can aspire to. To forgive is to release and to free the firebird to soar to its heights of love.

Song of Summer

I call to you, the weary and the careworn.

Come rest within this sweet haven,

And bathe in waters scented with flowers gathered on a

June day.

Gather of the light,

Gather of the peace,

Gather of the healing,

And rise as a flame of love,

Ignited by spirit power.

Chapter 4
The Yi Spirit of Earth

Attunement Meditation

The Spirit of Compassion and Sharing

Travelling a little further along the ebbs and flows of the rivers, oceans, springs
and fountains of light,
You now enter a place of such welcoming and such calm.
A place of centring and belonging.
You find yourself longing to reach firm ground and to tread upon the soft
contours of this rich and fertile land.
You long to rest in quiet valleys amongst the cool soft breezes and mellow
shade,
To run laughing to the summit of gentle hills,
To spread your arms wide
And embrace all that is,
All that has been
And all that will be.
With a song of 'I Am' springing from your lips, you at last know your purpose,
your place.
This is a time for calling back the whole of you,
The exhausted and exalted,
The disillusioned and dynamic,
The broken and the unbounded.

"I Am!" calls yourself back from the known and from the unknown.

"I Am!" rises as a clear and potent declaration.

It calls to your spirit as a being of earth, and to God as divine light and Goddess as the manifesting mother of all.

You are whole, and holy in your wholeness.

Strong, clear and free, you flow with a new compassion and clear intention of your purpose.

"I Am," you cry from such a depth of knowing that it spans time and space, encompassing all that was, all that is, and all.

The Yi Spirit of the Earth Element

Spirit of Bounty And Sharing

Late summer, or harvest, teaches of the infinite abundance of the earth, of the spirit of fairness and equality needed to provide enough for everyone. Often likened to a generous mother, or the divine feminine, the yi have the task of bringing life through into form and providing the nourishment and nurturing needed for growth. The yi is the spirit of manifestation and is found in the magic of drawing your hearts desires into materialised form in this physical realm. People with a strong yi often have little difficulty in forming the life that they want and need. The yi teach of the integrity needed to stand for higher values, and is the spirit of connection, companionship and caring. Yi in its highest resonance, flows with loving empathy, connecting all of life with the healing grace of compassion.

What do you dream of manifesting in your life?

The Essence of Earth Power

The essence of power of the earth element is to stay centred, and from this central core of knowing, to extend both inwards and outwards with deep compassion. Yours is the potency of intention, the magic of manifestation, as you see that thoughts become generated into reality from the seeds that are planted in the realms of becoming. Your power is that of connecting and holding, and then flowing outwards into life.

The Harmonious Resonance of Earth

Season is late summer or harvest.

Colour is yellow or gold.

Sound is singing like a lullaby, bringing comfort and caring.

Aroma is fragrant and sweet and can be cloying.

In the body, the earth element governs the digestive system, stomach and spleen, the muscles and overall shape of the body, the limbs and the sense of taste, thoughts.

The qualities invoked by earth are trustworthiness, thoughtfulness, caring, sharing, compassion, balance, co-operation, manifestation, holding and support, gratitude, bringing to fruition.

The Disharmonious Resonance of Earth

Overthinking, over responsibility, needy, ungrounded, density of thoughts, self-centred, craving, obsessive, stuck.

Symptoms – Digestive issues, heaviness and aching in muscles, prolapse, varicose veins, obsessive thinking and worry, issues with fertility and menstruation, migraine, headaches.

Awakening into Higher Consciousness

(The Resonance of the Soul)

Compassion as an all-encompassing flow. It starts from the centre of the self and flows outwards, holding all of life and acting as a bridge of blessings from difficulty and suffering towards higher intention and lighter purpose. Blessings in the realm of earth are the higher learnings and 'aha' moments when struggle and difficulty is overcome, and your light path emerges before you and around you.

Song of the earth element

The mother calls to you –
'Awaken your song of life
Dance and spin yourself into beautiful form,
Within this web of magical light.
You are light and you are form,
Bringing the blessings of abundance to all who understand and dance your
Ways of harmony,
Ways of balance
Ways of compassion.
Free yourself to dance to you highest tune,
Bringing fields of grace as
Healing'

Late Summer (Harvest)
Season of Earth

We arrive at harvest time, or late summer, the season when the earth element is at its glorious peak. Warm golden sunlight and softening energy perfectly expresses the generous and expansive spirit of the season. The landscape overflows with nourishing food and life begins to slow down a little, finding its own way and its own pace. People gather to eat the fruits of their labours; crops are harvested, and fruits picked from trees and bushes. The land gives of its bounty.

This is often a time of constant activity as food needs to be stored while the weather holds. In contrast to spring, when energy is high and creativity and activity rises to meet it, late summer, although busy, has more of a feeling of responsibility. What has been produced, must now be cared for properly so that people's needs may be met.

The Earth element is an expression of abundance and plenty, where needs are satisfied, the glorious promise of nature is fulfilled, and stories and laughter pour forth as bellies are fed and store cupboards replenished before the colder days begin once more. Nature sings of her harvest, and of reaping what has previously been sown in fertile ground. Wasps and other insects become 'drunk' with sugary fruits and time seems to dawdle, as this phase stretches out. The landscape is golden with ripe crops in the fields and long grasses singed to gold by the hot summer sun, now a memory.

After the heat and highs of the summer, this season offers a welcome break in intensity bringing a sense of holding and stability before the descent into autumn, followed by a further descent into the deep cold of winter. Late summer is the phase of connection between the rising of the powerfully creative energy of spring and summer (yang) and the falling into decay of autumn and winter (yin). Days are warm and mellow, and energy is stable and equable, feeling almost timeless in character.

The Earth element as the element of holding, and bridging has a particular role in the flow and changes of the seasons. In addition to its own expression, it creates the connecting field between each season, in effect holding everything together as a whole.

How the Earth Element Arises in the Body

Earth resonates with the centre of a person, with community and sharing, and with the digestive organs, stomach and spleen, which have a primary role in the distribution and assimilation of nourishment throughout the body. These two meridians of digestion run up and down the front of the body through the digestive area. The stomach meridian begins below the eyes, travelling down the face and head, around the mouth and descends down the front of the body ending in the tip of the second toe. The spleen meridian travels up the body from the inside edge of the big toe, through the instep and up the inside of the legs. It then travels through the digestive area, ending in the ribcage at the side of the body.

The stomach meridian travels from below the eyes, passing by the nostrils and mouth, suggesting that pleasure in eating is not only related to taste, but also comes through the colour and texture and smells of foods. The natural sensuality of earth energy loves to explore life deeply through the physical senses, absorbing pleasure from experience. Earth is concerned with taking in, digesting and assimilating on all levels of being, whether it's food and drink as sustenance for the body, or whether it's information and knowledge as sustenance for the mind, or pleasure as sustenance for the soul.

People with a weak Earth element often have trouble with their physicality and may have a weakening of the muscles or a weakness in the organs of assimilation and digestion. There may be a weakness in the tissues of support and holding, for example in the context of people who experience a prolapse of the internal organs. This may be prevalent in mothers following the growing and the holding and then the birthing of their infant. The Earth element has become weakened through this profound and fundamental effort and shows signs of distress through, for example prolapse of the uterus or the inability of the bladder to hold water efficiently.

This propensity can also be observed in people who have developed varicose veins; the veins have lost their power and musculature needed to 'hold' and have begun to collapse. Areas of emotional, mental or physical collapse may also be seen to indicate a profound distress in the holding nature of earth. Bring to mind again the mother who holds her infant no matter what. This 'no matter what' is a profound gift of earth and can be seen in any aspect of life where endurance, dedication and strength is needed, whether in a person, the power of the enduring landscape or the strong foundations of a building.

In a person, strength and endurance alone is not enough, but can be what is needed and called upon in many circumstances and life challenges. A strong earth creates a strong structure and musculature, including the muscle of the heart. The limbs are governed by the Earth element, and this is revealed through the muscular strength needed to 'hold' with the arms, and also to 'hold' what you care about with loving compassion. People with leg problems may have issues in relation to walking their path with confidence and standing their ground. The energetic phase of earth is about to taking the time needed to digest, assimilate and enjoy your path and the process of life itself.

People who carry the qi of earth have tones of singing in their voices which beautifully express the harmonious nature of the element. Much as a mother soothing a fretful child, the sound that they make is lyrical, soothing and lilting, echoing the rich song of life.

This harmony is indicated through the strong resonance between mind and body. Thoughts that arise from a settled mind and a pure heart create connective pathways between the inner and the outer landscapes. It is through these connective pathways that your thoughts become 'real' and manifest into your life. Thoughts have a power and a life force of their own, making it important to use this power wisely. Just as the food that is taken into the body creates physical health, so the thoughts that are taken into the mind create mental and emotional health. It is important to develop an awareness of the thoughts and feelings that make up your internal world and to understand that they will become mirrored and manifested in the outer world.

The powerful essence of earth
is to manifest that which is initiated
in the creative landscapes
of thoughts and feelings.

Earth teaches understanding. With great patience and endurance, it teaches that who we are on the inside, will manifest into who we are on the outside. How often do we hear that to change our life, we must first change ourselves? It is the power of intention, for good or ill, that governs the development of our lives and constantly manifests and re-manifests in a continuum, providing the perfect opportunity to deepen our understanding of this natural law.

The simple teaching is that if we don't like what happens, then we must understand our part in creating it, whether on a personal or more global and humanitarian level. Earth relates both to the individual and to the collective. What is in one, is in all, is the law. This law is echoed in the body. What is in the thoughts and emotions becomes manifest in the body and in the life around the body. The contours of the inner emotional landscape are revealed in the contours of the physical body. The Earth element not only oversees the musculature and the shape of the body, but also the whole of our physical incarnated being.

Just as the planet earth keep spinning, and life keeps moving, and nourishment keeps circulating through the body, there is a sense of constant activity in those people with a strong affinity with earth, Often unhurried, or moving at their own pace, they always seem to be 'on the go', whether caring for other people or caring for their own realms of responsibility, the movement carries on.

Contemplation for
Healthy Earth Energy

Give your legs a stretch and then a gentle shake.
Stand upright and relaxed, your feet shoulder width apart.
Take your attention to your lower abdomen.
Imagine, a stream of qi flowing down from the centre of your abdomen and into your legs and feet.
Imagine golden roots growing from the soles of your feet and anchoring you deeply within the earth.
See your roots flowing downwards through the darkness of the soil, through the rocks and stones of difficulty with confidence and a sense of ease.
Your roots travel right down to the centre of the earth and there connect with the heartbeat of Mother Earth.
The enduring timeless rhythm. Comforting. Nourishing
Holding
Feel yourself connecting.

Now imagine drawing a spark e of this essence up towards your physical body through your bright and golden roots.

See the golden roots still strong and firmly gripping the earth as the energy of earth flows strongly through your feet and your legs, giving strength to tired muscles and vigour to the body. It finally finds its resting place within chalice of your abdomen.

Take a breath and feel the strength, confidence and the lightness of being fully connected to the earth.

This will help you to stay rooted and centred, giving you inner stability. Practice regularly to help you to align with your authentic path in life.

The Yi Spirit of Earth

Does Your Story Reflect Your Higher Intention?

Late summer sings of the stories of life. The Earth element is the phase of energy that gives life to thoughts and dreams, bringing them down to the 'earth' of reality. It is about manifesting what was dreamt into being by your creativity (hun spirit) and joyfully fed with excitement and passion (shen spirit). The yi spirits sing of bringing heaven down to earth in glorious manifestation. If the hun spirit of spring is the creative idea, then the yi spirit of late summer is the architect of the idea.

The realm of earth is this incredible world in which each one of us lives, creates, evolves and discovers who we are. It is the realm in which choices can be explored and changes made to better reflect the person we are and are becoming. The element of earth gives us common ground, uniting us all on this planet with every other life form, as beings of the earth. It teaches of balance, fairness, trustworthiness and equality, enough for all. Consider the intricate balance of the ecosystems, all existing in their own realm, yet reliant on the balance that sustains them all.

A key resonance is trust, and the spirit of earth will prompt questions about trust. On a broad scale – can life be trusted to continue? On a more individual scale – how trustworthy are you? And do you trust life to support you? The yi can be trusted to create and provide everything that is needed for the continuation of life in all its varied aspects. The earth element is the nourisher, sometimes called the Great Mother who nurtures and supports all forms of life in an endless spiral of giving.

Imagine the yi as a spiral of light, flowing through and encompassing the entire planet in a loving embrace.

As love arises from a strong and pure heart, the energy of earth moves it outwards as caring and nourishment towards life in a greater sense. The flows of qi start with the centre and move towards the periphery creating a spiral of moving energy. Originating at the centre of self and moving outwards is the direction of the spirit of earth. The yi teaches that to help and understand others, we must first help and understand ourselves.

Meditation to Connect with the Spirit of The Yi

Bring to mind a spiral of light emanating from the centre of your body. Imagine it to be golden and warm, like rich honey, circling and spiralling through your body, but with its roots firmly within your abdomen. Allow yourself to relax completely, and with this deepening relaxation, comes the deepening of your breathing. Let your breath be like warm golden honey, flowing in spirals through your body, finding its own rhythm, finding its own way. Your golden breath and your golden light naturally come together. Blending and flowing, they begin to create a deeper rhythm and a deeper harmony within your body.

Feelings of pleasure and warmth arise naturally. Allow these feelings to flow gently around the whole of you, and through your limbs to the outer extremities of your body and beyond and into the space around you.

Imagine the spiralling light, creating circles around your body. See the warm golden colours and feel the light permeating and filling the space around your body.

Watch it flowing naturally outwards, reaching deeply into the earth and spiralling high into the heavens creating a beautiful network of light.

You are held, and completely safe within this spiral of light. All cares and worries now become transformed by the light as though they never existed. Feel the deep pleasure of being free from concern, free from conflict, and at peace with yourself and all that is…

Gently draw your focus back towards your body, towards the rising and falling of your breath, returning softly to your own centre and allowing the spiral of beautiful light to wind its way back towards your abdomen.

There it roots and settles, giving power and light to the whole of you and connecting you with the power and light of your own life.

Take a few moments, allowing yourself to return fully to the present.

Worry – Emotion of Earth
Can You Move Beyond the Contours of Your Emotions?

When life throws challenges in our path, it is natural and appropriate to experience feelings of worry, but problems arise if worry is always allowed to take root. When worry is the first port of call, or the instinctive response to life's challenges and up and downs, then earth's natural resonance of balance and harmony becomes disturbed.

Worry can naturally arise as an appropriate response to the difficulties that we all encounter, or it can be a more profound and habitual response to life's ups and downs. Worry often renders you incapable unless it is supported by constructive action. There is a saying in Chinese medicine that to ensure healthy Earth qi, every thought must be balanced by an action. If worry and anxiety spin around your mind and body with no resolution or activity to overcome it, then health issues may arise as the 'holding' power and strength of the yi become overused and tired.

This more entrenched and habitual response may arise from a deeper level of trauma and imbalance, where the internal equilibrium, or solid and reliable ground, has been deeply disturbed. It can arise from an over-zealous need to be 'good enough' and the overriding need for personal recognition. Worry is the lower emotional state of the Earth element and can compromise and erode a steady sense of balance and wellbeing, destabilising the sense of grounding and place in life.

Emotions of worry, fretting, fussing and anxiety can take over, like weeds taking over and choking the land. The internal landscape changes to reflect this, and constructive 'fertile' thoughts and feelings may become choked and overrun by the weeds of dark and heavy thoughts and emotions.

When working in my own garden, I make use of this idea, so my work becomes something of a spiritual practice. I have huge amounts of brambles and nettles, and as the brambles cling around my clothes, scratching and tearing at my skin, I often equate them with clinging and tearing emotions and thoughts as I systematically clear the land once more, knowing that as I do so I also clear my internal land. I watch how bindweed nettles and ivy quickly take over, if allowed free run, choking other less robust plants, and find these realisations very helpful in my quest to remain unchoked and clear in thoughts and intentions. I also understand fully that I need to keep clearing the land, and that this realm of earth is a realm of repetition. We must keep repeating our actions. A house is not cleaned just once, laundry washed just once, or a garden weeded just once! In the same way, we must keep checking in with our thoughts, emotions and intentions – it is not a 'just once' practice.

Many turn to food as a solace for worry, and comfort eating is something that most of us have taken refuge in from time to time. Food be used as a personal punishment or reward, and many people have an emotional connection with the food that they eat. An instinct of the mother is to feed her child, but when out of harmony, this same instinct can overindulge or deprive, and our 'internal mother' can make use of food in this way. Eating disorders can arise from a level of instability and insecurity, often developing in childhood. When distressed, many people rely on sweet, sugary, comforting foods as a pick me up. Sweetness is the flavour of the Earth element, and people who seek the 'sweetness' in life may turn to an inadequate substitute in terms of sugar to temporarily feed their internal emotional state of need.

Insecurity can arise in many ways, creating difficulties in making choices, as every aspect of life becomes chewed over and fretted over. "Which food for the senses, nourishment for life to choose? How to make life sweeter?" The spirals of qi become embedded and circular, and rather than spiralling outwards, towards life, become a never-ending, tight spiral around the worries and concerns that catch the attention of the emotions. Thoughts spin around the mind as a mirror of this flow. 'When to help self, and when to help others?' is one of the huge questions that can be a much-encountered dilemma for people with unbalanced flows of Earth qi. There is often a great sense of care and responsibility and these people desire the best outcome for all, finding it almost impossible to put their own needs and desires above others.

Choices can become a great source of difficulty, making decisions fraught with dilemma. "If I do this, then perhaps this could happen. If I do something else, then perhaps…" and so on. The internal conversations are worrying and endless, with the result being an internal knotting of thought and energy where what could be straightforward choices and decisions become huge mountains to climb. The mind goes from one situation to the other and back again, which can be extremely tiring and frustrating, as there is no fulfilment of a smooth and powerful choice. The phrase being 'stuck in the horns of a dilemma' perfectly illustrates this arena of emotion and thought.

Can you choose and stay centred in the power of your own choice?

The path of the soul is not one of worry, but one of balance and fairness, sometimes requiring the individual to put their own needs first and sometimes the needs of others. This creates a beautiful and dynamic spiral of light and equilibrium. Try to keep a lightness around making choices and decisions. Nothing is final and there are always opportunities to make further choices and decisions along the way.

Divine help comes from the lighter flows of earth, which tells us not to worry, that there is infinite energy and love available for all. Higher streams are created from the compassion and empathy that is so natural for earth as a healing power. This flows above and beyond the worries and concerns of everyday life and out into the fields of grace, where it is available for all. Strong and flowing earth energy brings about a sense of contentment, commitment and trust. No need to rush or to fret, all concerns, worries and needs are taken care of.

Contemplation to Ease the Distress of Worry

Take some quiet time alone.
Place your hands gently upon your abdomen.
Pour loving words and praise into yourself.
Become aware of any resistances, such as I don't deserve, or I'm not good enough.
Continue to flow pure love through and beyond these wounds.
Allow the release of your emotions as you gently hold yourself.
Let go of all those who have hurt you.
Let go of all situations and circumstances when you felt embarrassed, belittled... not good enough.
Call upon the spirits of compassion to cleanse your wounds with gentle healing love.
Keep returning to this place until you have released and forgiven.
Breathe in new energy, feeling the strength of the earth beneath you, supporting and holding you through all the difficulties that form part of you, and which help to manifest the contours and shape
that is the whole of you.

Earth Element as Goddess

In many cultures the world over, the earth is depicted as Goddess, with her role of birthing, engendering life and providing food and nourishment for all in her care. The spirit of earth is strong and generous, not differentiating the needs of one from the needs of another. In her eyes, we are all the same, and she endlessly gives of herself, fulfilling the essentials of food, shelter and all material and practical requirements. Given the right care and conditions herself, she will openly respond by producing an abundance of everything that is needed for life on earth.

We are dependent upon this bountiful mother, who provides the very ground on which we walk, the soil in which crops are grown, and the materials from which we build our homes, places of work and the many other structures we need for shelter, education, industry and places of culture and worship. The needs of modern humanity are great and are placing unsustainable strains upon the resources and goodwill of the mother. As we evolve in complexity, our needs as beings of earth have become greater and more complex.

The qi of earth as Goddess holds everything together, providing the balance and equilibrium needed for each phase of growth or change to flow into the next. At times of imbalance, she will find the balance, at times of change, she will create the bridge of movement from one phase to the next. Humanity has faced many desperate times, but it is this beautiful earth that sustains and allows the continuation of life and the opportunities for rebuilding and for new choices and new beginnings. She also has her own season of fulfilment at harvest time when her abundance is birthed and pours forth, but perhaps her greatest task is holding everything in place. She arises in people, who have the balance and equilibrium to hold things together through times of turbulence. This is a great gift, and one which I have come to know as 'walking the middle ground' (please see contemplation for Holding the Middle Ground that follows).

Chapter 5
Holding the Middle Ground

Take Some Time to Study a Yinyang Symbol

The light side of the yang and the dark of the yin are equally proportioned and balanced within the sphere of the whole, one flowing into the other in a continuum, neither more nor less important than the other.

Each holds an element of the other, a circle of dark within the light and a circle a light within the dark, indicating that each carries the potential of the other, and nothing is fixed or absolute, but is created out of movement and change.

The line between the light and the dark forms an 'S'.

Imagine walking along this line, holding the light on one side of you and the dark on the other.

As you walk the path of your life, hold the two aspects of yin and yang, light and dark in full awareness and in equal balance.

One is incomplete without the other, and each generates the other in beautiful harmony,

One the sun and one the moon.

It is in the holding of both that our completeness emerges.

Consider the strong foundations that are needed for buildings and structures, such as roadways, bridges and other constructions. Consider the strong foundations of a mighty root system that huge trees need in order to stay strong and steady. Consider the huge strength of the land upon which life grows and structures itself. Consider the strength that can be needed to create strong and reliable foundations for your own life in order to weather the storms that can blow unpredictably through your world. The ability to consider is a power of earth, as consideration leads to understanding, which gives everything its place or position in life. Earth qi is ordered and structured, keeping the equilibrium, which could be called the 'middle ground'.

The Earth Element out of Balance

When You Lose Your Footing

Concerns of an earthly nature can be seen in the unfairness that still exists across the globe. Earth as qi of balance and equilibrium is compromised through human levels of unfairness. The compassion of the mother teaches that all are equal, and all must have their fair share. However, life is often at odds with this sense of balance. There are those who have too much and those with too little.

The qi of earth holds a mirror to reflect the dangers and imbalance of over consumption, and the overly complex needs and cravings in the individual. The Earth element in a healthy state is balanced, steady, stable and has an easy flow, with resonances of giving and receiving both being generated in equal measure. If giving and receiving become unbalanced, then the energy can split and become unsustainable. It splits into divergent streams of unhealthy qi which tend towards either giving or receiving, rather than the harmony and balance generated when both are equal.

The energy that flows out towards life will then reflect this split, and the internal harmony of earth in the individual becomes compromised. This can be seen in the overconsumption of information, food and products; having to 'know' and having to 'have' may result in an unsustainable pressure on the Earth element to keep receiving and receiving, and consuming and consuming.

In a person, this disharmony in earth can lead to a sense of bloating and a lack of fulfilment, where nothing is ever quite enough, and 'something else' is always drawing the senses. This takes us right out of the present moment into an imagined future where everything may appear to be 'just right'. However, the power of earth is to hold the present moment and make use of past experience and future hopes as fertile ground for manifestation.

What really matters to you?

Contemplation for
Giving and Receiving

As a gentle healing, bring to mind a figure of eight, with each side balanced and flowing both towards and then out of the other.
The figure of eight can be used in meditation and contemplation as a way of understanding your own energetic flows of earth.
Are both sides equal?
Does the giving side equal the receiving side, or is one side bigger than the other?
Imagine and intend them to become of equal in importance in your life.
As one flows into the other, so giving and receiving become constant, and ultimately the same.
By taking the step of creating the intention of balance in your life, things can start to change and realign within and around you.
Flow the figure of eight in gratitude outwards towards the spirit of the earth for all that she gives to you.
Flow it out with compassion as a healing intention towards creating a more balanced and sustainable way of living on this earth.
Flow it out with love and gratitude for all the blessings that you receive and that grace the path of your life
As you flow it outwards, you will then perceive it flowing inwards towards you alive with blessings and gifts.

Moving into the Shadowlands
of Earth

Unearthing Your Hidden Power
to Manifest Your Dreams

Let's jump into the trenches and dig out 'Poor Me'. As the energy of yi is explored within the shadowlands, this could be termed the negative aspect of earth, where emotions are split, powerful and embedded in the past. Sometimes ungrounded and scattered through denial of self, or conversely deeply entrenched, immoveable and overly concerned with the self. Both these ways indicate deep imbalance and create inner divisions and difficulties. It becomes almost impossible to move on in life, as you have become stuck in the mud of the past. The energies of unbalanced earth are centred in difficulties around the sense of self and place in life. These difficulties and the insecurity that emerges from unstable earth arise as 'I want', or 'I don't want'.

Emotions can be self-centred, opinionated, self-important, putting 'self' at the centre of everything. "What's in it for me?" Or "how does it impact on me?" Me, me, me. More, more, more. There is deep and entrenched dissatisfaction, unfulfilled cravings, and here is to be found the dark pathway into the realm of the obsessions and possessions, emotions and cravings making the qi tightly spiralled inwards towards the self.

These people can become untrustworthy as they wrestle with this constricted and dark inner world, being consumed by cravings. The tightly bound earth ego finds it difficult to release these bondages of cravings in this material world as it is packed with 'treats' and temptations – the hungry ghost wants them all!

In Chinese medicine, this kind of endless craving is recognised as a pathology, and in extremes, these people are termed 'hungry ghosts', always wanting but never satisfied. In the classical texts, it was said that after death these hungry ghosts walk the earth plane, tied in an endless spiral of longing. They are starving and wasted, mouths open wide and eyes as pools of endless darkness. They missed the gifts that they were given in life, becoming needier and less satisfied regardless of what was offered. Their spirit was unable to receive and learn the grace of gratitude. Enough was never quite enough...

At the other side of the circle is to be found the polar opposite. 'I count for nothing,' or 'I am barely present in this life' or 'I exist only to fulfil the needs and cravings of others'. 'I am Cinderella, always the servant and never the princess.' These people are often anxious and depressed, their feet seeming to barely touch the ground. They may look a little translucent as they strive to become incarnated and present in their own life. It's difficult for them to feel very much or to make choices or firm decisions, because they feel unimportant and as though they barely exist, so ingrained are the needs of others before self.

Their constant worrying becomes a kind of mental craving as the answers they are looking for are always just out of reach. What they think they want keeps shifting and changing like an illusion. Life never seems to work for them, and this sadly feeds into their belief that they 'don't deserve' or 'don't count'. They can feel deeply inconsequential. 'I really don't matter'.

This kind of imbalance can lead a person to becoming overly needy and craving of sympathy, as the very earth beneath their feet feels vulnerable and untrustworthy. They may crave understanding and support beyond what is reasonable, feeling clingy and insecure. Conversely, the distress may be on such a deep level that sympathy and care is spurned as in their eyes, the world cruelly rejects them and as a mirror they reject the world in return. These people 'bunker' themselves in as a protection against being hurt, potentially becoming overly independent and overly self-sufficient and preferring to walk their path alone.

When a person is either dark and unmoving, or ungrounded and anxious, a tight spiral of restricted energy flow is created, possibly leading to many difficulties. This spiral creates difficulties with both giving and receiving. In some instances, there seems to be a one-way flow, of either giving or receiving, but this is always is eventually mirrored back by life. The yi spirit is about fairness and balance. "What is given is always received," it sings, and this energetic creates a continuum until something comes along to change it. In terms of an image of earth, it is like digging over the same patch of ground again and again; you may need to expand your horizons if you want something different.

Sympathy is an emotional resonance of earth, and though this can be a wonderful and appropriate gift to offer and receive from a state of balance, it can also become a craving. People with a deep imbalance in the Earth element often crave sympathy above all else as they gather stories of how badly life has treated them and how difficult things are. These stories are used to extract sympathy from other people, over and above what is appropriate.

Earth on the Rise

Loosening the Spiral and Becoming Abundant

The yi spirit of earth moves in circles and spirals of qi. It flows with ease and grace, encompassing all in its path. This is reflected in a healthy individual, the spiral of qi emerging from the centre as a spiral of light, encircling the physical form and flowing out into life. If this circle is large and expansive, or tight and restricted, this can be seen reflected in the attitudes of the individual. An expansive yi can indicate a large and generous sphere of influence, whilst a diminished yi can indicate a very limited scope.

This spiral is reflected and mirrored by life and can be experienced in what is given being mirrored by what is received.

As Earth qi begins to expand to encompass larger perspectives, the internal landscape alters, and you can now 'get out of your ditch' and make strides to build your confidence. At this level of rising energy, a sense of responsibility emerges towards manifesting something good for your own life, and you may begin to believe in your dreams once more.

Climb out of your ditch of difficulty and walk the path of your desires and dreams.

As qi begins to move outwards, changes can take place. You can begin to believe in yourself once more, becoming strong, stable and trustworthy in your energy, helping you to gain stability in relationships and all other aspects of life. Life becomes easier and more comfortable. As you begin to understand that how you think and feel manifests in your life, then this knowledge alone is enough to prompt many people towards the task of changing their thoughts about themselves, to a more expansive, supportive and positive outlook.

Holding yourself in the grace of compassion,
and let the past be the fertile ground of learning
from which your present and your future grow.
Plant only the seeds that you wish,
after careful consideration,
To nurture and nourish as seeds of your life on this earth.
Feed them and foster them with attention,
Taking the care to understand their needs.
Dig out the choking roots and weeds of heavy emotions that threaten their beauty and unimpeded growth.

There is an acupuncture point that I frequently use to help patients who have the archetype of earth. It is to be found at the side of the ribcage, and if you were to hug yourself, then your fingers would naturally fall there. Think of it as a warm and loving embrace from your earthly mother (Goddess). It is a place of deep nourishment and spiritual stability and encourages a deep and loving acceptance of yourself just as you are. With acceptance comes a security of spirit, and a new phase of growth emerges through becoming more confident in the making of empowered choices and decisions.

Deeply accept yourself just as you are.

People who carry a strong element of earth are generally both loving and deeply compassionate but have a wonderful practicality which urges them to care in an 'earthly' sense and to do and to give what is needed. Under this archetype can be found people in the medical profession, complementary therapists, teachers, carers, social workers, as well as chefs (earth loves food, remember), those in the building industry and engineers (strong structures and foundations). To fully encompass the spirit of earth is to be practical, knowledgeable and resourceful. The spirit of yi seeks to understand how things work and is hungry for information and for experience. Earth just loves detail 'How does that really work?' They love information, both from the sense of gathering knowledge, and to give themselves a sense of where they fit in with life. 'How?', 'Why?', 'When?'

A strong affinity with earth gives the capacity to be consistent and able to endure life's difficulties with grace, dedication and empathy, which coupled with a sense of the practical can greatly help in the ability to think fruitfully and make strong decisions. Challenge a person with a strong yi, and give them a problem to solve, and they will find the answer. Being the information gatherers, they will research and discover what they don't yet know. The spirit of earth encourages and fosters the dedication needed to understand, both in a practical sense and in a compassionate sense. In a broader more spiritual sense, the questions asked of the yi are 'How does life work?' and 'Where do I fit in?'

Earth folks have little trouble walking in another person's shoes and can feel deeply for this other person. We can go overboard in our willingness to understand and we may inadvertently fall into the pit of difficulty with that other person, such is the level of worry and concern. When this happens, there are two people in the pit instead of just one! In a state of equilibrium, it is possible to support a person through their difficulties with the grace of empathy and the strength of compassion without losing our own centre and sense of self. This can take practice and means developing a strong core and sense of who we are. From this perspective, it is important that the care and concern for other people doesn't lead to a sacrifice of you or me, but leads to an act of empathy, service and compassion, where all benefit, and not one at the cost of another. This phase of energy is about equality.

Can you dig deeply within and give of yourself
as a grace and not as sacrifice?

Developing a sense of self and the understanding that you are an important part of the balance and flows of life on this earth is very grounding and enabling. Every life is part of the integrated dynamic of earth, and it is important to find a sense of this inside yourself.

Understand Yourself

Understand what matters to you in life, in terms of values and attitudes, and try to follow these through in all situations. If you say you will do something, then try to fulfil this promise. Promises must be fulfilled in order to keep the sense of centre and the sense of integrity in balance. Having personal integrity is crucial, to this energetic phase, as integrity is what holds everything together, integrating all aspects into a whole. A strong integrity is a quality of earth and holds the body, mind and spirit together. Integrity is the stuff that holds families and relationships together and keeps you centred, strong and grounded.

As this phase of energy becomes higher, lighter and less 'earthbound' or entrenched, there is a rite of passage which can be tricky and prove hard to navigate. This is the landscape of appearing to care, and indeed being helpful and concerned, but secretly wanting something back. A tricky landscape to navigate is the – 'If I do this for you, what will you do for me?', which on the surface may seem perfectly fair, but in the deeper recesses of shadow, hide the cravings of 'wanting'; 'I want reward to ease my cravings. Look at me! See how wonderful I am! After all, I've done for you…!'

Although the self is beginning to give and is sincere in caring, there are heavy conditions attached. This means that the centre is not entirely genuine or strong enough to be sustainable, creating tension between the energy of giving and the energy of receiving. Here the split is still visible, and this inner conflict can be tiring as the thoughts bounce between genuinely wanting to give and secretly wanting something back.

Beware of the little martyr hiding in this landscape, whispering, "It's okay, I don't count, take what you will of me, I know I don't deserve very much. I'll place you on a pedestal so that you can exploit me. Oh, how I suffer for you." Underneath in this shadowland lurks the ego, smug and self-satisfied, "Look how wonderful I am, look how much I give. I think I'm a saint, or perhaps an angel from heaven. I'm little Cinderella amongst the ashes of my own dreams, burnt on the altar of other people's needs and arrogance. Poor me!"

Tricky landscape indeed, as on the surface you appear to be giving and selfless, yet you are still deeply attached to your neediness which leaks into your ability to be altogether open and genuine, making you feel unhappy and unfulfilled. You crave attention and want to be noticed for your selfless goodness – you have a gaping wound in your centre, whose story is 'If I give enough, surely I'll eventually be noticed and showered with gratitude and gifts.' This dynamic of energy plays into the religious and spiritual life as 'If I'm really good, then God will shower me with gifts and give me everything I want'.

The journey for you is to heal the gaping hole, in your centre by understanding your genuine needs and caring for yourself enough to feel a sense of fulfilment. You may find yourself face to face with a call for honesty as you look more deeply within and acknowledge how you really feel, rather than how you think you should feel, which is often laced with the burdens of guilt.

> You are important, and how you feel is important.
> Take the time to care for yourself,
> To understand yourself,
> To gather knowledge about yourself,
> To know yourself.

It is time now to address and release that guilt. Guilt is a merciless master, and will keep you in its claws, shaming and tormenting you all your days. I urge you to examine your conscience and to address everything in your life that has led to you feeling guilty and responsible for another's pain. The urge of the yi is to take steps to put things from a sense of responsibility and balance, and through this, to release the difficulties that accompany guilt.

If you are not able to take these steps, then resolve not to repeat past mistakes and understand how guilt controls and manipulates you. You can then use your power of choice to decide whether you wish this to continue or whether you are ready to move away and beyond its clutches, saying a firm 'No' when it raises its head. Guilt is like a trip wire and serves no purpose other than to make you feel horrible inside.

Conscience and a sense of responsibility are a different matter and have their place as a guiding force over what words, thoughts and actions are healthy and what are not.

Intention as Healing

I had reached a point in my life where I became acutely aware of the hurt that I was responsible for and of the imbalances in the dynamics of some of my friendships and relationships. I had fallen into the trap of being an 'appeaser', and just wanted to make people feel happy or better in some way, which as a long-term strategy can never play out into healthy relationships. I knew that I could not make further spiritual progress until I had healed this karma and created healthier and more balanced dynamics with the important people in my life, and with my own integrity.

With this in mind, I set the intention of healing all the relationships in my life. This empowered prayer that I sent forth took me on many paths over some years, all of which were spiritually directed and guided and not 'set up' by me. My responsibility was in keeping my prayer alive and in my genuine desire to heal friendships and relationships where things had become tricky in some way, or out of balance, and ultimately to heal my relationship with myself.

On one occasion, I was thrown into the company of my first husband, and the whole experience had the flavour of a 'set up', or, in other words of being divinely directed. We arrived separately in Thailand to visit our son, who lives in Chiang Mai, a large city in a Northern province. We found that we'd booked into accommodation at either end of the same street. I knew something was afoot, as this could not be a coincidence. I started to seek my ex out, even though he was doing his best to avoid me. We kept bumping into each other and I was aware of the help around me and sensed a strong spiritual presence, encouraging me to take the right steps.

I understood that here was an answer to my prayer and took the opportunity to insist that we meet for a coffee (my treat, the only way he would agree!). Although I had not had an agenda for our conversation, I found myself deeply apologising to him for being young and foolish enough to hurt him. We were both tearful and he also apologised to me. The space between us became clear and we then spent the next two weeks happily in each other's company, something that neither of us would have believed possible. Such a miracle of grace and blessing.

This same prayer has led to the near break up of my present marriage as the difficulties between us rose to the surface to be addressed, balanced, forgiven, and released. It led me to begin standing my ground with people who had been taking a little too much advantage of me. It led to me training as a soul healer as a way of both healing my own very deep hurts and helping others on a path to do the same. It led to me reaching out to friends with whom I had lost contact. It has led to me having a clear and loving relationship with myself, and to a deep acceptance of life as a reflective mirror, and of my own place within this.

The prayer continues its resonance in my life, and keeps me on a steady path of balance, helping me to think and act from a space of compassion and awareness. If I forget to do so, even in everyday ways, such as careless patterns of unhelpful thinking, or slipping into the swamp of heavy emotions, then this prayer becomes active and I find myself balancing things out again. The prayer also leads me to looking at both friendships and working relationships in a new light and stops me from falling into the old familiar pit of 'I don't matter. I'm only here for you'.

This prayerful intention has become an active miracle in my life for which I am truly grateful. I have a greater sense of wellbeing and more available energy, as I have reclaimed myself from negative contracts and made an attempt at turning them into positive contracts, where everyone gains. I am free of the 'need to be liked', and what a freedom that is.

The power of intention is such a guiding force. If you send out prayers and statements with a strong intention, or we could say, a strong spirit of yi, then they will become answered, and many things may change around you as life answers your cry. Some of the events that took place around me were quite complex, and quite obviously divinely led. I would often throw my arms heavenward in disbelief. 'How did you do that?' I would ask in awe at how life responds on such a level. I have thanked my angels, guides and helpers so many times for 'setting me up' so that I could heal my relationships and my life – they are the same thing really, as one reflects the other.

Prayers are always answered, maybe not in the ways that we would like or that are easy for us, but if the intention is sound, then they take us to a better place. This healing has freed me from any guilt I was carrying for words unsaid, or hurtful things I had done out of my less-conscious, less-formed self. My relationships feel genuine and balanced. How incredible is the synchronistic web that creates the opportunities that we ask for, and I walk this web of light with a sense of wonder and, always, gratitude. As we become lighter and more balanced, so the life and relationships around us take on the same resonance acting as a profound and clear mirror.

This mirror reflects your intention. It asks, "What are your deepest intentions towards life? What do you now see reflected back towards you?" The spirit of earth teaches that what is given shall be received and what is received shall be given in an endless dancing spiral of balance.

The Resonance of Earth Is Balance
and Acceptance

Take every opportunity that life presents, to understand yourself more fully,
more deeply.
How is it that you habitually feel?
What are the thoughts that forever stop you in your tracks,
the emotions that sink you deeper into the quicksand?
Take time to look within, and when the opportunity presents itself, allow any
heavy feelings or discomfort to rise into your conscious thoughts so that,
without judgement, you know them and recognise them.
Set aside the need to repress or disown any part of yourself, but in this moment
fully accept yourself as you are, and as your life has shaped you.
Become familiar with your light and your shadows, and perhaps one day you
will see them all as helpers and friends along the way.

Perhaps you too are at a point where you are ready to set the intention of
healing your life. It can be quite an undertaking and may include people and
events long forgotten that need a level of care, understanding, balancing or
healing. When you begin this journey, do so with an open heart and mind and be
prepared to follow the guidance when it comes. At this point, you do not know
where it will lead you, but it is a wonderful means of learning about yourself,
along the way, and of growing into a new and more expanded way of being.

No longer the need to hide from yourself, as you are now committed to
healing your past, which creates more energy for your present and your future,
and releases people, circumstances and events from the restrictions of being

buried in old guilt or emotion. Self-knowledge is an essential aspect of awakening to higher realms of awareness, and when you know yourself, life becomes easier and more comfortable, as you no longer need to hide in the ditches and mud of a poor sense of self.

Awakening into Higher Consciousness

These higher and finer realms of qi are where compassion as a constant state of being is created.
In these realms, feelings of frustrated craving and selfish desire have long since drifted away and been replaced by feelings of gratitude and wonder at the blessings of life.

Blessings can come in many guises. They can be beautiful and magical gifts but can also be the difficulties through which something is finally learnt and overcome, where a sense of compassion emerges for the you that has struggled and wrestled with problems and difficulties, and with others who wrestle with the same. Understanding is key to the domain of earth, as is the dedication needed to achieve this level of compassionate understanding. In essence, a need of earth is to be understood, but the journey begins by developing a deep and authentic knowing of yourself.

Extending this same care to other people, and out towards life as a whole, creates a spiral of energy. Understand yourself, and this will be reflected back to you from the understanding that is offered in return to you by life. This in itself is a mighty task and part of the awakening into the higher consciousness of the earth element invoking a higher level of being. Authenticity is a key to the essence of the spirit of earth, which asks, "Who are you really beneath the disguises that you wear?"

Earth spirits teach that the more authentic we are with ourselves, the more authentic we can be with others, creating a deep core of inner stability.

No longer the need to hide,

but to hold yourself in the dancing light of compassion

As we rise higher into these realms, the blessing of gratitude is revealed. To flow with gratitude is to be open and emanating in your compassion towards life. Gratitude is a blessing of thanks which earths you. The more earthed you are, the higher you can extend without drifting away.

Thank you for my beautiful life.
Thank you for today

A spirit of gratitude towards life and towards everything and everyone, who is important to you, not only keeps you fully alive and present in your own life, but also helps to keep the things or people you are grateful for present in your life. Without a spirit of gratitude and appreciation, things and people can float away and out of your sphere of reality.

A vital stage of inner development comes with the ability to balance and master the emotions so that you are not controlled by them but acknowledge their presence. No longer are you swayed by the emotional cravings in yourself and other people and are able to respond with empathy towards genuine needs. As higher and more refined spheres of energy flow light through the emotional body, you realise that healthy human development embraces understanding through relationship, whether the relationship is with another person, or with your sense of self and your own life. You can now encompass all with your expanded self, and the 'either/or' of the denser flows of qi is now replaced with a true understanding that what is given to one is given to all.

Relationships create a clear mirror through which we can view ourselves. The energy that extends as thoughts, feelings, beliefs and attitudes is reflected back through the people who are closest. The spirit of yi is above all, gentle, kind and genuine, striving to understand itself through understanding others, and this is the foundation of the awakening of compassion as a powerful and radiant stream.

In this space, you will begin to feel such a deep radiance as the flows of compassion are created from within the depths of your soul. You will care for yourself in the same loving way that you care for others and for life, and this creates spirals of light and healing with the resonance of compassion. Consider again the figure of eight. Both sides are equal and balanced, and who knows where it begins or ends. Some traditions name the figure of eight as the number of the Goddess as it signifies the continuum of life and the balance and equality of giving and receiving as a beautiful and sustainable intention.

Compassion is the highest virtue of the earth element
as a spiritual emanation and is the substance that unites us all, with each other,
and with other forms of life.

A Meditation for Gratitude

Take a moment.
Inhale and exhale deeply.
Bring to mind all the people in your life who you love and feel a wave of gratitude sweeping from deep within your soul and reaching out to them.
Bring to mind the people who challenge you or with whom you have some difficulties.
Feel a wave of gratitude sweeping through you from deep within your soul and out towards them for all that they teach you about yourself.
Take a moment to release all negative bonds between you and offer them the grace of forgiveness.
Think of your life and all the experiences, difficulties and pleasures that have made it what it is and that have formed and shaped you into the person you have become.
Send out a wave of gratitude from deep within your soul for all the blessings in your incredible life, and for this beautiful planet earth.

Manifestation as a Grace of Earth

Make a list of all the good things you would like to manifest into your life. These can be anything at all that matter to you. Keep the list close by where it can catch your attention, and as you read through it now and again, 'fire it up' with some powerful gratitude. If you remember, gratitude helps to 'ground' the things that matter to you.

Gratitude works like a thread of magic, drawing things, events, people and circumstances towards you. Notice and be grateful for how these threads weave and spin in a network of magic in your own life. Begin to see what appears as opportunity or gift and then do what's needed to follow these threads. Life will always respond, but very often in ways that we could not have imagined.

Now make a list of the inner qualities that matter to you so that with practice they may become materialised as your intention and purpose.

What qualities do you admire in others that you would like to foster in yourself?
What feels authentic to you?
What are the callings of your soul?

It can prove challenging to learn to become and to embody higher states of being and it is reasonable and understandable that although we may occasionally 'hit' these highs, few of us can sustain them, without dedication and practice. Dedication is a high quality of earth and is the magical thread that binds desire to intention.

A higher frequency and resonance means that changes take place on a deep and subtle level. While this is in process, you will come and go between this level of being and lower and perhaps more familiar states. This is where your own deep compassion for your own self and the journey of your soul must come into play. Over time, these higher frequencies of qi will begin to flow through your meridian system emerging outwards through your mind, body, spirit and out into your life as beautiful rivers of light. They will also flow deeply within, taking you to new ways of ease, abundance and fulfilment in your life.

Become Compassion

It is in this phase of light that we learn to 'walk our talk' so that our actions match our words and our thoughts, and the whole of us begins to come together and move through life as an integrated embodiment of higher consciousness. To be whole is to have a vibrant sense of self, with no aspect left out. You welcome the whole of yourself and fully embrace all that you are.

It becomes easier to know what you stand for in life, and to hold your ground over the things that have meaning for you. Your thoughts and feelings will become aligned with the compassion of a greater and higher intention, and your life now moves with a sense of ease and lightness that once seemed impossible to achieve. Your intention becomes manifest, with ease and grace.

"Yes, you do deserve, of course, you do," sing the spirits of yi.

It is now the moment to spiral into a strong connection with your higher self, casting off your old dance of the undeserving. As you care and nurture others, this comes back again and again as blessings of grace in your life. Look for the detail, the kind words, small gifts and gestures that come to you. Perhaps the things that you once held dear or the desires you once had, no longer hold sway over you. You may become open to different possibilities as the depths of your soul become manifest.

Hold out your arms to receive,
and
Let life pour its gifts upon you

Be open to receive, and allow yourself to claim your own life, your own self and your own way, with the same level of unswerving compassion that you extend to others. Let go of the 'either/or' that previously consumed you – 'either you or me' expanding into a greater capacity of 'everyone'!

I am the dancer in my own earth life

Move and dance with the grace of one who 'knows', as your learning has been great and varied upon the paths you have trodden, and in your knowing, hold a space of compassion for others who walk their own paths.

Becoming compassion as a beautiful witness of life unfolding but rooted and held by your own power of knowing. You are enough, you hold the chalice of compassion of a life lived through the power of deep and centred learning.

A Prayer for Life

Sit with ease.
Relax your breathing, allowing it to find its own natural path.
With eyes open, but gaze soft and gentle, look outwards as though into your own life.
Imagine a glorious golden sun emitting its radiance from the centre of your being.
Feel the warmth and sense the brightness as it becomes stronger, emanating from deep within the core of you.
You are deeply at one with yourself and your own life journey.
All that you are, have been and will be, could be, may be, is centred here in this profound and peaceful moment.
Enjoy the moment.
Enjoy your earth path
Enjoy dancing with life.
May you be blessed all your days.
May you find the pathway to your Soul.
May the Spirit of Compassion flow through you.

The Po Spirit of Metal

Attunement Meditation

The Releasing Spirit of Autumn

Our journey through the waterways comes to rest at last in a magical place of
beginnings and endings, endings and beginnings.
Here a resting place.
Here time to slow everything down, and here hide from the tumult and
cacophonies of everything your life has been, could be, may be…
Here the air is light and vaporous, rising in wonderfully oxygenated clouds.
Take a long slow breath.
And then another.
The air is so pure, so rich, like no other air you have tasted.
It fills your lungs, flowing through your body.
Scattering your thoughts like leaves on the wind, it, blows through your tired,
tired mind, tossing away the unwanted, the unresolved.
And then peace.
Such deep, deep peace.
The world is quiet now. Air moves gently through your senses like a tender
breeze, loosening ties, loosening bondages, loosening the past, loosening hurt,
grief, wounding.
As if following a higher force, the healing breeze flows through to neglected
places, dusty, cobwebby places, dark crevices where demons lurk, hidden.
The breezes flow on and on to a forgotten part of you which now breathes,
stretches, yawns, awakens, as if from a faded dream.
So long buried, you thought it dead, you thought it gone.
Your animal nature wakes. Wild instinctive, protective.

Always right.

The Po Spirit of the
Metal Element

Spirit of Release

The Po spirit of Metal (or air) is the instinctive, protective nature. Po is the spirit of release and is the ultimate judge of what is right, and what wrong, what good, and what bad, what to be held and what released. As the spirit of refinement, and the one that calls you to a realisation of what to must be let go of, and what held on to as learning and treasure for the soul. The po is the spirit of the physical body, in Chinese medicine, called the corporeal soul, and journeys through the shadows and mysteries of what is deeply hidden from normal view and only sometimes revealed. It will urge you further into your own inner dark, helping you to venture into the deepest abyss of yourself. It will bring you the rich treasures of purity, beauty and courage as your pain and suffering is transformed through the light of awareness.

Do you have the courage to really let go and release the past?

The Essence of Metal Power

The essence of power of the metal element is the absolute courage to hold the matrix of past and future as strength, foundation and learning. Yours is the realised self-esteem, and yours the sword-like courage, to completely release all that no longer serves your higher purpose and stand in the silence of being. Through the release comes the inspiration of the new, the refined, the precious and the beautiful, as pure gifts of soul.

The Harmonious
Resonance of Metal

Season is autumn.

Colour is White.

Sound is the weeping of grief and loss.

Aroma is of rotting leaves.

In the body, the metal element governs the lungs, the large intestines, the skin, the immune system, and the sense of smell.

The qualities invoked by metal are purity, release, refinement and the letting go of what no longer serves with the courage to see this through to the ultimate death of the old.

The Disharmonious
Resonance of Metal

Depression and grief, low or inappropriately high self-esteem and self-image, isolated, hoarding ghosts of the past. Vengeance through an inability to 'let go' of past slights or wounds. Vague and otherworldly. Longing and regretful.

Symptoms – Irritable bowel syndrome, constipation and other disorders of the bowels. Issues arising from imbalanced self-esteem. Asthma, bronchitis and breathing difficulties. Skin conditions such as eczema and psoriasis, rashes and dryness.

Awakening into Higher Consciousness
(The Corporeal Soul)

The willingness to let go of and to 'die' to what is not longer of value, going beyond the confines of personal grief towards the creation of sacred space for the treasures of soul. The courage and the instinct to journey into the 'Great Silence', where truth prevails.

Song of the Metal Element
(also named as Air)

Metal heralds the well-defined death of the old,
When life withers and makes its return to earth.
There is no choice – this is a natural part of The Way, the mighty cycle of life and death, death and re-birth.
It teaches of separation, of letting go and leaving behind.
With metal, there is clarity – anything that is not of value must be eliminated.
The sharp definition of the sword creates a strong boundary.
Metal teaches that everything has a beginning and an end, a birth and a death.
Each breath that you take has its own beginning and its own end…
A birth and a death.

Autumn
Season of Metal

(Also Named Air)

And so to autumn when nature begins her glorious descent. As if in showy defiance of the loss to come, leaves are at their most startling and beautiful before

164

they fall. Autumn creates strong definition, trees emerging stark and awkwardly stripped of their warm rich colour. Earth begins to gather all of this beauty towards herself and to reclaim what is rightfully hers for the creation of fertile ground for forthcoming seasons of growth. After the exuberance of earlier seasons, the magic and grace of autumn has a dignity and magnificence that almost takes the breath away. There is a sense of loss, of happy halcyon summer now a fading memory.

Some people feel a sense of mourning at this time of year, as the stories of summer become a dwindling dream and what was once new and vibrant growth ends its cycle and diminishes. Qi withdraws, and the landscape quietens down. Autumn can be a time of intense feelings of loss as the vitality and high levels of summer qi give way to quieter flows of energy. Natural forces slip towards their descent. Autumn highlights contrasts and can mark a sudden and well-defined change from soft and equable late summer. The descent can be slow and gentle, or it can be sharp and fast. The stability of languid late summer can no longer be held, and everything must fall away.

The change and refinement of autumn is the herald of a new loveliness which of itself is a powerful gift. The beauty of descending qi is subtle and gracious and a contrast to the ascent of exuberant summer. Consider the infinite beauty of soft morning mists and spider's webs, intricately woven and hung with diamond drops in the early morning light. Consider too the jewel-like colours of trees as they display their finery, before finally letting it slip away. The sun hangs low in the sky highlighting the soft beauty of the fading landscape.

The natural world is exquisite in contrast and colour as it heads into the death realms of the year. Acting as a mirror of the diminishing forces of qi, the soul creates its own beauty. Becoming introspective, it instinctively draws inwards as a reflection of the shortening of days, the lengthening of nights, as the cycle of the year naturally comes to a close. People may echo this change of tempo and welcome the opportunity to take a breath and to slow the pace a little before the final descent into the depths of winter where the flows of qi can sink no lower. This is a time for remembering the cycle of the seasons and for storing up resources against the forthcoming cold.

Can you breathe to the edges of your being…?

Breathe...

Take a deep breath, feeling it filling your body.
Gently let it go
As you sit, stand, lie, breathe fully into this moment
Embrace the physicality that is your body and sink inside a little more fully, a
little deeper
With every exhalation, softly let go of all the moments that are not this
moment, and be here, fully committed to knowing yourself a little more.
A little more lovingly.
A little more joyfully.
As you take another full and miraculous breath, imagine every cell in your
beautiful body awakening to the cry of life as if for the first time,
responding to the call from your deepest,
wildest self.

How the Metal Element Arises in the Body?

In the body, the metal element oversees the efficient elimination of potentially toxic waste. The lungs and large intestines as organs of elimination are under the auspices of metal, as are the skin and the nose, including the sense of smell. When all the possible goodness has been made use of by other organs and processes in the body, then what is left is no longer of value and becomes potentially toxic and hazardous. It is the large intestine that governs this process, and its coupling with the lungs may not at first appear relevant, but the qi of metal talks of the double process of both taking in purity (fresh air) and releasing impurity (body waste). The spirit of metal teaches of purity and impurity and of having a strongly defined sense of both.

The lungs are the organs of breath, and breathing is so essential to life that few of us even recognise that we are doing it. It is so instinctive, that we only know we're doing it if it is compromised in some way, for example if it is restricted, perhaps, through lack of available air or through a condition of the lungs such as bronchitis or asthma. As we breathe in, we have the gift of life. As we breathe out, we release the waste that is not conducive to life, and this profound but simple rhythm continues from our emergence into this world to our departure. This reveals the relationship with the Metal element to life and to death. It is defined and, in these terms, simple.

The lung meridian arises in the chest, indicating the special relationship between the lungs and the heart. Both heart and lungs create their own rhythms within the body and support the process of life as we know it to be. The first point on the lung meridian is just beneath the collarbone, where the chest meets the shoulder. The flow of the meridian is down the front of the arm, ending at the outer edge of the thumb.

Breath is imperative to life, and we cannot survive for more than a few moments without the taking in of oxygen and the release of carbon dioxide.

Can you breathe to the edges of your being…?

The lungs inhale and exhale through the nose, and conditions such as stuffy noses and blocked sinuses, asthma, bronchitis and other breathing complaints all fall under the jurisdiction of metal. In people with a weakness in metal, the sense of smell may be compromised. Smell is such a beautiful sense and can invoke a huge array of feeling and memories, often long-buried. Do you remember the smell of freshly cut grass? Does it take you back to your childhood? Do you like the smell of petrol, of fresh paint, or the scent of roses, lavender or freshly washed laundry? The sense of smell can whisk us away on the wings of memory and fantasy, evoking strong emotional responses. It forms part of the instinct. We 'know' when something smells good or bad and is potentially healthy or harmful.

The large intestine is the major organ of elimination. It teaches the lesson of releasing and letting go finally of what is not needed and what is potentially poisonous, purifying the body of toxic waste. There are many diseases of the intestines in our world, whether cancer, colitis, irritable bowel syndrome and other irregularities in elimination. The large intestine urges the release of contaminated thoughts and behaviours as well as physical waste from the body. Constipation, for example may be an indication that something on the emotional level needs to be processed and released. Are you feeling particularly 'uptight' about something?

The large intestine meridian arises on the outside edge of the index finger, travelling up the arm neck and finishing on the face just to the side of the nostril. There is a much-valued and frequently used acupuncture point called The Great

Eliminator. It is sited along the large intestine meridian and is to be found in the web of skin between the thumb and first finger. It can be profoundly helpful in the release of migraines and headaches which have arisen through excess emotion, stress, overthinking, overeating or from generally inefficient elimination. It is also thought to be helpful in the treatment of all conditions in the upper body, as well as conditions of the intestines, such as constipation, hence its rather grand name of 'Great Eliminator'. Try massaging this point with a firm pressure for a minute or two, to alleviate headaches, migraines and indigestion. It can be used as a tonic, along with deep breathing, to help in stressful situations and to increase feelings of wellbeing.

The Metal element governs the skin, both as a physical boundary and also as an eliminator of toxins, for example, facilitating the release of sweat through the sweat glands. The skin is the largest organ in the body, acting as both a defence against invading bacteria, viruses and so on and as a protective and weather proof boundary for the body. It is the point of separation between self and others as it delineates the physical being. The overall health of a person can be seen in the condition and lustre of the skin, and issues of self-respect, emotional eruptions or internal pollutants can emerge as skin complaints: rashes, eczema, boils and pimples etc. The skin acts as a huge sensory organ. Have you ever felt your skin 'creep' when you're frightened, or felt your hairs stand on end? It is an organ of instinct and is always accurate in its perception.

The instinct is there as a protective ally and the Metal element teaches of the need for a strong boundary as defence against invading forces and pathogens. In acupuncture terms, it has an important part to play in the strength and integrity of the immune system. This is indicated in its governance of what to take into the body as being pure healthy, and what to release as toxic or unhealthy. Given the right environment, the body has an extraordinary capacity to 'correct' itself, or to 'right itself', and metal is the element of balance, of right and wrong. It teaches the immediacy of releasing what is wrong and a threat to the continuance of life, and giving value to what is right and an enhancement to the continuance of life.

The element Metal arises in people as its own language and like all the elements can be heard, seen and detected through feeling, observation and sense of smell. In the skin, it arises as a white hue that seems to float like a mask just above the physical skin. There is a feeling of purity and stillness around these people, perhaps even an air of holiness or reverence in the more religiously or spiritually inclined amongst them. There is often a silence, as though this person has removed him or herself to another world. The voice has a catching or 'breathy' quality, which speaks in tones of loss or regret, sinking and falling away at the ends of words or phrases as through there is not quite enough breath to sustain what is being expressed.

The aroma that arises is of vegetation rotting on a woodland floor, or sometimes a mustiness or dustiness like the leaves of an old book or a long-forgotten attic room. The energy speaks of loss, of grief and of regret, and sometimes of a higher aspiration towards another more beautiful realm. There can be a 'rock-like' quality, as if frozen in time, grief and loss holding a person in a fortress of inertia as feelings become locked away.

Metal also has a certain resonance with the mind. Thoughts can drift across the mind like wispy clouds of air, shapeless and formless, and require a foundation to give them texture and meaning. They require context and emotion to empower them. Of themselves, like air, they have nothing. To focus on the present time is to have a sense of presence in the world.

Take delight in your own ability to breathe.
Listen inwardly to the flows of air coming and going within and around you,
Listen with reverence to the breath that sustains you in this world.
Give a little time and space in your daily life for this simple and profound
practice.

The Po Spirit of Metal

Do You Have the Courage to Let Go?

The spirit of the metal element is the po, and its teaching is of purity and quality. With the po, there are no excesses, and at this point in the cycle of qi, no life force wasted on anything that is not of value. The po is the spirit of the animated body, sometimes called the corporeal soul. Animal-like in its instincts for life, it connects to the wilder side of us, the side that knows how to protect itself and protect loved ones. Its way, in this regard, is clean and simple – to live or to die.

Autumn teaches of the wisdom of releasing all that no longer holds merit, letting it fall and die away, so that all that remains are the exquisite jewels and treasures of a life well lived, and that which is necessary for the continuum. Why be burdened with clutter, whether of mind, body or spirit? Memories of the stories of the cycles of growth and change that have been lived and the deeper learning that this living has inspired are stored away as treasure for the developing soul.

Autumn, with its air of mystery and melancholy, invites a change of pace, the chance to slow down and to reflect on what really holds true as having lasting merit. This phase can also herald a new beginning, with schools and colleges starting their new academic year. There is a freshness in the air as a different level of qi emerges and natural forces and temperatures fall. As qi descends from heady heights of summer and the holding stability of late summer, this new phase can call to you as an individual, helping you to separate from the crowds and to find your own impetus for life. You may feel inspired to follow a quest to discover fresh opportunities or to make different choices and reset your boundaries.

The energetic shift after the endless and even flows of the qi of mellow late summer, can be awakening. This is the energy of sorting and sifting through your choices over how time and other assets, including your valuable life energy, are spent. With the ending of the year, comes the realisation that individual resources, including life, are finite, and this often stimulates the desire to reconsider the more profound and significant personal questions. This phase of metal calls on the need to re-define, re-evaluate and to seek more deeply, perhaps uncovering gifts and attributes that have lain dormant and buried beneath other pursuits and activities. Uncovering the depths of who you really are can significantly help towards the building of your self-esteem by creating a wider, higher and deeper, and potentially more enduring, sense of your individual value.

Just as the po spirits teach of personal value, self-esteem and self-respect, they are also the teachers of truth, and the courage that is sometimes needed to be truthful in your thoughts, words and actions. The metal sword with its defined and clear edge offers the clarity of insight needed to cut through, the sometimes subtle or deeply hidden webs of lies and deceit, and to arrive at your own clearly defined boundary of truth and the truth of who you are as an evolving soul. Even small untruths can build upon each other and before long a rabbit warren of distortion has emerged taking you away from the jewel of your soul. Truth creates strong boundaries. If you can define truth within your own self, then you will have a strong level of honour and self-respect, also qualities of the Metal element.

What qualities of being
does my soul wish to express in this lifetime?
How can I perceive and give definition to these qualities
within myself?
Can I recognise honour, courage and respect as my qualities of truth?

Light Breathing

This breathing exercise is wonderful to do at the beginning of the day, or just before you go to sleep, bathing the whole of you in gentle healing light and taking you to a quiet place within where the voice of the soul can make its presence known.

Lie comfortably, making sure that you are warm enough to completely relax.
Allow your body a little time to soften, giving it permission to 'let go' of the day that has passed, or thoughts of the day yet to come.
Rest your attention for a while upon your breath, becoming conscious of where each inhalation begins, and each exhalation ends.
As you relax further, pause slightly at the beginning and end of each breath, feeling your lungs gently expanding and contracting.
Begin to visualise breathing pure white light into your lungs, seeing it spreading further and more deeply into your body with each breath.
Visualise, and sense the white light pouring down your spine and throughout your whole body, flowing through to the surface of your skin. See it hovering above the surface of your skin.
Imagine every cell to be responding and resonating with this healing energy.
Take the light through to any physical aches or pains and feel these areas gently restored and relaxed.
Flow the white light out through your heart into your life and towards any struggles or issues that you may be experiencing.
Visualise all difficulties being healed and transformed through this pure white light.

Imagine this pure white light flowing strongly outwards and encircling the whole of the earth, bringing the purity of healing to suffering.
See the whole planet enveloped in the purity of peace.
Start to gently draw the light back towards yourself. Take your time to allow your awareness to fully return to your physical body, and your surroundings. Have a gentle stretch before either settling down to sleep or carrying on with your day.

Many people with a strong Metal element in their elemental makeup find it difficult to cut away the past and are filled with regret for what once was and is no longer, for opportunities lost, or for happy times now a fading memory. They often try to hold on to the ghosts of the past, finding it difficult to let them go and to hold them in the heart and soul as treasured memories. A confusion can arise about what is of the past and must be released, and what of the present.

What am I doing with the life that I have?
Am I happy?
Am I fulfilled?
Who and what is of value to me?
Do I live amongst the clutter and ghosts of times long gone?
How do I spend my precious life force?
Do I need to make new choices and let go of some of the old ways…
Then with the next breath,
I challenge myself to begin my new ways!

The po spirits teach of gathering tightly together and refining. All excess is removed or released and only the beautiful and the pure is retained. The gems, crystals and precious stones that we are all familiar with, some of them exquisite and valuable and worn as signs of status, or given and received as tokens of love, come from deep within the hidden contours of the earth. Changes in temperature and intense pressure over long periods of time eventually create objects of great value and beauty, some of which are thought to possess qualities of healing. There are many healers and lightworkers who use crystals for helping people, and who are able to deeply understand the differing qualities of these precious stones in their treatments.

And so it is with the qualities of the individual soul. The spirits of po will work at refining and shaping your inner being by means of the many and varied events and situations, the emotional experiences and perpetual learning that life offers. Though the seasons of time, the passions and storms of intensity and through loss and gain, all excess will be released and discarded; the jewel-like qualities of the individual soul emerging radiant, beautiful and strong.

Grief – Emotion of Metal

The downward Force of Release

The emotional life of metal speaks of grief and loss. Just as surely as birth is a natural part of life, at the other end of the natural scales lies death. The bereavement over the loss of a loved one can leave deep scars. Sometimes these never feel truly healed, as loss is a very difficult phenomenon to encompass. Perhaps the best we can do is to find somewhere to place these losses, and somehow build the structures and edifices of life around them, but the depths and profundity of our nature means that we never truly forget.

The 'never-forgetting' can mean that fortresses are constructed from deep within as structures of protection against deeper feelings. They are formed from the stones and rocks of frozen emotion. Time seems to stand still in these inner places, as though the breath of life itself is being held. Nothing moves respires or changes. Time needs to be given to all these deep and complex feelings, and this can be a very natural and much-needed part of recovering from the tearing and often seemingly cruel blade of loss. However, problems arise when too much energy, or life force is invested into the construction and maintenance of these fortresses, when living within this fortress becomes a way of life rather than a protective ally. Like the fabled *Princess in a Tower*, what was once a protection can sadly become a prison.

The natural processes of life can help to restore a person once more, and the internal emotional weather conditions experienced over time can see the eventual crumbling and return to earth of these protective or prison-like structures, making the invested qi available for 'something else'. Imagine ivy growing over and around your fortress and the winds and rains of emotion, and heat and light of the powerful sun of love, eroding the rocks and stones as a natural and healing process. Metal teaches of the balance of loss and gain as weighed upon the scales of life. Experience and life events can create and re-create us, and as beings of a malleable substance, we hold the potential of allowing the force of courage to re-shape and remould into a more refined, more defined and encompassing version of our former self.

Many of us have experienced what happens at the times when with a thin veneer of courage, we set out into life, thinking that we have our pain and grief tucked away and under strict control, then unexpectedly someone breaks in with offers of sympathy or kindness, 'I was okay until you were nice to me!' The warmth of another person can melt the frozen fortress allowing healing waters of tears to pour freely as a release. They were only just beneath the thin surface. The more deeply rooted fortresses can take more time and more warmth to gently ease them away, dismantling them stone by stone until the courage and confidence to rebuild has been found.

There is another form of grief, and this is the grief over the perceived loss of your own life. You feel that you have in some way, or over the passage of time, compromised or given away, or had taken from you the substance of your own life. This is a grief that speaks of opportunities lost and potential never realised, and this form of grief can lead to a dark and deep anger over the injustice. You want your life back. You want another chance. 'If only I had had the courage to go for it, to break out, to step away, to claim my own self!'

This can be painful and difficult to manage. However, another chance is only a breath away. Another chance to breathe into your own life, releasing everything that does you any injustice, or renders you inert. Another chance to change and to shift your outlook and beliefs from unhealthy dynamics and relationships that impose upon you, to something lighter, more aligned with the truth of the soul. A chance to breathe new life into your own journey of becoming the incredible being that you truly are, giving air and wings to your dreams and aspirations.

The lungs teach of breathing deeply, not only on a physical level, but of breathing fresh air into emotionally charged situations, including how you feel deeply within yourself. Breath creates space, and the inspiration needed to resolve tight or difficult circumstances. The lungs also teach of boundary – how deeply can you inhale? How far does your exhalation extend? Deep and wide breathing improve the health of the whole body, sending oxygen to the organs and tissues, and creating free and open space for the revelation and release of deeply held emotions and beliefs.

There are two stages to the following breathing technique of release and renewal. It is my own version inspired by ancient yogic practice. I have found this breathing practice moves energy and releases emotional stagnation and toxins very rapidly. Please give yourself time and clear space around this practice, making it a daily part of a purification ritual. As you enter more deeply into your hidden self, you may find that your preferences for food change and that you need a fresher and simpler diet for a while. Please drink plenty of fresh clear water to help with the purification and elimination of bodily and emotional toxic waste.

Breath of Release

To prepare, sit in a relaxed upright position. Allow yourself to become
physically relaxed, but with a mental attitude of clarity and focus.
Breathe deeply for a few moments while you find your point of awareness.
Now begin to consciously expand and contract your lungs.
Begin to pant with short and light in and out breaths through the nose, having
the lips gently closed.
As you continue for a few moments, encourage the muscles in your torso to
become activated as part of your breathing.
Now, focus the panting breath within your lower belly.
Next, take a strong breath in, tightening your lower belly and as much of your
lower body, including your legs, as you are able to.
Hold this breath until you need to let it go.
Release the breath and at the same time, release the holding and tightening of
your lower body.
Relax and take a pause at the end of the exhalation and become aware of how it
feels to be still and empty.
Repeat three times.
Return to a natural way of breathing.
Become your own witness to the new feelings in your body and your mind.
You may wish to spend a few quite moments in meditation or contemplation as
you assimilate the changes that are taking place within you.

Stage 2

As you become more accustomed to this powerful breathing technique, begin to visualise your mind as being pure, clear and filled with light, allowing this clarity and light to flow through your body with each exhalation.

Metal Element as Judge

Metal is the well-defined realm of right and wrong, good and bad and wields the final word of authority as judgement over what is just and what is fair. Within this arena are the lawyers, barristers and judges. They decree what is right and what is wrong under the auspices of our laws, maintaining the matrix of responsibility that oversees the upholding of the strong principals, ethics and morality that govern our society. The police exist to enforce the integrity of the law acting as a protection against wrongdoers. Metal is also the realm of the armed forces of land, air and water as protection against invasion.

There are people in this energetic realm who deeply desire peace and justice in the world such as those who work for human rights or other activists for positive change. This is the realm of the idealist, and those with the inspiration to see and feel how life on this planet 'could' be. Here also are the heavy metal bands, the singers and the metalworkers and mechanics. This is the realm of technology and instant communication. It is also the realm of spiritual aspirants, priests and religious leaders and inspirational speakers.

The Metal element teaches of separation and the courage to leave something behind. With metal, there is clarity – anything that is not of value must be eliminated, recycled, let go of, there is no value in clutter, excess or the unnecessary. The sharp definition of metal gives people, events and situations a strong and definite boundary. Think of a metal blade with its clearly defined edge. The spirit of metal teaches that everything has a distinct beginning and a distinct end, a birth and a death. There are no uncertainties or blurred edges. It teaches that now is exactly the right time to cut through illusion and to cut away the stories, actions, thoughts, emotions or attitudes that perpetuate suffering. The Metal element encourages strength of character and the resolution needed to forge new or strong values and to reset boundaries. Metal is the spirit to stand up against what is perceived to be wrong and to assert what is perceived to be right.

The Metal Element
out of Balance

When It's Hard to Let Go…

The teaching of the po spirits of metal are centred around the appropriate release of what is no longer of value, and the retention of what is pure, true and good. They teach of the value of retaining only the treasures of learning as cherished riches of the soul. When out of balance, this process goes awry. This can be seen in everyday life as the archetypal hoarder. Everything is kept, treasured and stashed away 'in case it's useful' at some point in the future. This imbalance can also be indicated in the individual who keeps nothing, consigning all the treasures and mementoes of times gone by to the rubbish heap. Both these two pictures are extreme and can be seen mirrored in the large intestine as overly slow evacuation, or indeed constipation and the toxicity that accompanies this, or at the other end of the scale as very loose and frequent evacuation with the release of valuable nutrients.

The other major organ under the governance of the Metal element is the lungs. Imbalance can be perceived in the person who barely seems to breathe, holding back in a perpetual state of retreat from life itself, and appearing almost transparent. At the other end of the scales is the individual who is overly present having no trouble at all in voicing opinion, whether valid or welcome. As the large intestine is responsible for the release of toxic waste, and the 'dregs', an imbalance in this energetic can be observed in the individual who has no respect for the power of words using foul, toxic and degrading language as a norm. Again, there is another extreme to this state of being, and can be found in the person who is overly cautious and careful and precise, holding back on a healthy flow of expression.

As grief is the emotional nature of metal, then the appropriate expression followed by movement through and beyond its strictures and ties demonstrates a healthy movement of metal. Again, for our example of imbalance, two extremes are cited. There is first the individual who cannot bear to feel emotion and blocks it from view with the rational and practical mind and a 'life goes on' mode of being. This person may have a very practical notion of death, seeing the release of the physical body as nothing more than as factual part of existence. At the other end of the spectrum is the person who simply is unable to move beyond their own experience of grief and tragedy and becomes forever locked into a veil of tears.

The matrix of the Metal element seeks to hold extremes as a strong foundation, using the balance of releasing and retaining as its scales in life. When the scales are tipped too far for too long, then imbalance begins to take root and finds its way into the structures and foundations of the individual. In addition to holding the balance of extremes, a strength and gift of metal is the capacity to think and act swiftly in order to retain the balance of right and wrong, good and bad, life and death. To vacillate or cogitate may prove to be hazardous in these terms. Think of an arrow with its sharp and clean trajectory heading swiftly towards its target.

Each breath I take releases me from the ties and strictures of the past.
Each breath I take welcomes the inspiration of the new.
The profound balance of existence builds a matrix of light for my evolving soul.

I am Pure
I am Light
I am Free.

Moving into the Shadowlands of the Metal Element

Exploring the Hidden Depths to Seek Purity and Courage

What do you give life to?
What do you give your thoughts to?
What do you empower with your own breath of life…?

Like a sword or an arrow, the Metal element in a clean and clear state of balance seeks to cut deeply through to the core of the innermost hidden depths and darkness. Of the unknown and the unseen, with its sword-like accuracy and its light of truth, it seeks to sever the constrictions of emotional toxicity and aggrieved thinking to clear the way for opportunity, renewed choice and the spirit of freewill. When the undergrowth of past grievance is cut away, clear space is created for the something different, and potentially something new and inspired.

By their very nature, the shadowlands of metal are well hidden from view. They are the depths that not many of us like to admit to, even to ourselves, and that can be because we can't see them, so buried are they within the gloom and ghosts of the past. They lurk, deeply hidden within the rocks and stones of our own grief and misfortune, and sit, boulder-like and still, blocking light from entering. They are so still and silent, brooding, looming. Here is the realm of the buried hurt and grief, stored amongst internal rubble as protection and armour against more hurt. The more buried we are, the less that life can hurt us…

The higher realms of metal provide the impetus to breathe air into this lower realm, to loosen its clanking and heavy chains, and shed a little light into the murkiness of past sadness and loss, past injustices. To dwell in this past is to become forever a victim, forever cut down upon our own internal emotional battlefield. The shadow of metal demands a vengeful justice, wanting to settle the scores of past injury and past injustice. Nothing can be released, nothing let go of, all is frozen in time, waiting, waiting, waiting for the final battle. As the blade of metal glints in the hand, where does it land? What is the truth of your pain? Who to blame?

What do you see when you look into the shining metal of truth? The sword of truth as a reflection of self is a sword that many people find difficult to wield, preferring always to look outside and to blame other people, events, circumstances, for all their suffering. The sword of Damocles is wielded over the heads of those who have hurt, betrayed, upset or disturbed us in some way, real or imagined. This sword of vengeance demands the heads of the betrayers and pain-bringers. Dark thoughts fester and dark voices inside our own heads demand 'justice' for those who have hurt us. This voice goes on and on, there is no end to it, no boundary until we make the decisive and final choice to end it.

This particular choice is a choice of power. The soul voice whispers in our own darkness that perhaps the way of revenge is not the path of light, but again and again, this is silenced by the judge and jury of vengeance who demand 'a head for a head' as justice! Again, the voice of soul whispers, unheard in the darkness. The rational and cruel darkness bypasses the gentle urgings of the soul and again craves 'justice'. The dark emotional self is demanding, loving nothing more than to dwell in the past, continually drawing attention to past events, past slights, past hurts. This is not to say that we have not all suffered and some of the suffering has been profound, affecting some people at very deep level of being. We find ourselves in the darkly emotional territory of the metal element, which is the realm of 'when your back is against the wall, sword in hand, what choice do you make?'

Do you listen to the voice of your conscience and the whispering voice of your own internal divinity? Do you listen to your mind reeling off images and memories of hurt like a film show? Where do your choices come from? What is the guiding force? Is it light or darkness? Good or evil? This is the realm of metal – the defined and clearly boundaried choice. Where you place your sword will have consequences. All actions, choices and behaviours have consequences. This is the law of life, sometimes called the law of karma. If you find it hard to make your choice, then look further. Take a little time and breathe before choosing. Become witness to your own self. Observe your thoughts, actions and choices. Look towards the future into the possible consequences of the choice that you are about to make.

Please consider deeply what it is that you allow to live within yourself and what it is that you consign to death? Is it the past with its sticky wings of darkness that you create and recreate in a continuum as you continue to remember and to feed the memories with emotion? Is it the courage to step into new life, into the unknown, into the wings of light? Where do you place yourself? You are more powerful than you realise as you now hold the balance within your grasp. Take a breath, and then another, and consider deeply before you choose. Make use of the breath as a stabilising source of energy. The breath with help to clear the mind, allowing for a deeper guidance to emerge.

Breathe

As we move to new territory within the shadowlands, a different story unfolds. Here is the realm of pious purity. This speaks of being so perfect, so impeccable that we are untouchable, and therefore beyond judgement by lesser folks. We are separated from others by our own perfection and are so special that we simply and effortlessly deserve all the treasures and wonders that life can bestow. This energy is fastidious, obsessive and can be very 'fussy' about what is liked and what is not liked, what is acceptable and what is not. This separation puts the self at the centre of everything that happens in life, as though life is somehow there to serve this person.

There can be a kind of glamour associated with this energy, as it demands quality and perfection, is often flawless and exacting. It often sees other people as 'less than', and those who are 'more than' are not welcomed into the personal sphere in case the need to be 'perfect' and 'the best' is compromised. Being the best and having the best are the exacting demands placed upon life. This energy does not 'suffer fools gladly', feeling itself to be superior and separated, but also putting the self under the unsustainable strain of continually reaching for and possibly falling short of these impossibly high standards of the ego.

There can be religious superiority within this realm, and a piety that becomes isolating and cold. An authoritarian and male god is wielded as a weapon to impose upon the lesser folks, and also to impose upon the self as severe judge. Here is to be found the god of judgement; heaven as a reward and hell as punishment. This authority is external, and represents something outside the auspices of the self, as being frightening and threatening. This attitude can also extend to other figures of authority in life (particularly male). These figures represent a judge whose standards can never be achieved. We always fall short, with the resulting damage to the sense of value and self-worth.

Conversely, there can be a complete denial of spirituality and the denial of any god, but particularly god as loving creator. In this instance, all creation and life itself are purely accidental unless explained and understood by the cool rational mind. This rational mind is 'the denier' seeking to sever all connections with what may lie beyond the everyday earthbound reality, preferring to live in the logical world of the five senses. 'If I can't see it, feel it or touch it, it doesn't exist.' Down comes the blade of severance as denial of the vastness of the mystery of the unseen, undiscovered and intangible.

There is also a realm of difficulty in the shadowlands of metal, which lives in the dark and mysterious realms of death and beyond. Here is the realm of phantoms and ghostly figures, the realm of the spirits of the underworld. People with this deep imbalance can appear 'haunted' and are beset by unseen beings and forces which far from being helpful, undermine their own progress in life.

Metal on the Rise

Seeking Your Innermost Treasures

The spirits of the Metal element speak of holding onto the past as deep and profound qualities of soul and as treasures of learning. On the other side of the scale, the po teach of rising upwards towards the heights of new inspiration for the creation of a lighter and more refined you. You are called on to notice the movements of the breezes and winds of change for growth and regeneration.

> Take a deep, deep breath.
> What inspires you?
> What do you aspire to be
> to have
> to do
> to evolve towards?

Just as they inspire through the higher rarefied realms of heaven, so the po urge the undertaking of personal and spiritual growth towards higher aspirations. While the journey into death and beyond is deeply honoured and acknowledged, so too are the spirits of life. The po hold past and future, life and death in a perfection of balance, neither one having more or less importance than the other. Respect is a higher teaching of the po, and the treasures of the known past and the unknown future are apportioned equal levels of energy, honour and respect. The po ask that you respect yourself and your own development and through your own levels of self-respect that you can offer the same to other people and their pathways of discovery.

Metal in a purified state wields the sword of its own internal standards of self-realised authority, which is by its very nature well-defined, and like a razors edge, seeks the clarity of a refined and disciplined mind. Clear and pure reality is like fresh mountain air to the mind and can help it to gently release heavy emotional states and the weighty rocks of the past. Practice perceiving your life as it actually is in the here and now. Consider the blessings and the challenges and weigh up what needs to be released or worked through to facilitate change. Where are your unshakable rocks, the solid foundations upon which you grow, and where your areas of rubble and decay that no longer serve you? What to keep hold of, and what let go of. As you let go, space appears for inspiration to arrive.

In the world around, rocks and stones are the external and visible structures of the Metal element. They are, unless subjected to extreme and unusual pressure, well defined, with a strong and clear boundary. They have stood the tests of time, being refined through the plays and pressures of weather and events. They stand still and enduring as a strong and reliable foundation. The very name 'metal' implies strength and foundation and provides the bedrock upon which life plays itself out. We like to say that we are going to 'test our metal', when life asks something that requires courage and endurance.

Try this simple breathing exercises as a way of releasing the intensity of stress and anxiety that may arise when your own foundations feel 'rocky', and your way uncertain or ill-defined. This breathing technique when practiced over time can create strong internal foundations, building legitimate fortresses of balanced self-esteem and the courage and confidence needed to face yourself and face the world. From the perspective of the Metal element, the external world is a balanced reflection of the internal world.

Abdominal Breathing

Sit upright but relaxed with both feet on the ground.
Relax as much as you can, lightly resting the hands on your abdomen.
Allow your breathing to find its own natural rhythm and gently let go of the outside world.
As your breathing begins to soften and your body relaxes, sink your awareness down to your abdomen.
Imagine it as a beautiful chalice.
As you breathe gently, begin to fill your chalice with energy and light.

Continue until your chalice of light is full and let it spill over and flow around your whole body.

Enjoy the flows of energy.

When you are ready, see the light returning to your chalice and gently come back to your everyday world, feeling refreshed, relaxed and energised.

Rising into the Realms of Light

Inner Divinity

The po are messengers of the male aspect of the divine, and take you to the point of an internal quest around questions about the male figures of authority in your life, and in particular about the position of God as father? How do you view your father, and God? As provider, as guardian, friend or advisor? As judge and authority? Very often, the way we view our parent is reflected in how we view the divine. Do you call upon this external God at times of extreme pressure?

In the teachings of the Five Elements, all is balanced and harmonious, and just as the po spirits teach of the divine patriarch as God, so the yi (spirits of earth) teach of the divine matriarch as Goddess, bringing about the natural harmony of yin and yang, both in balanced relationship with the other.

The journey of the soul is to move and evolve towards our personal balance and through this gateway, towards higher aspiration, with the balancing of male and female, yin and yang, spirit and matter within the personal journey of evolution. In order to achieve balance, we must be willing and able to have the courage to look deeply with the sword of pure truth and to see our own imperfections, and our own emotional rocks and boulders that can block lighter and higher flows of energy from view.

To make progress, we are called to take the courage needed to do just this. It takes great resolution to look into the mirror of blame and judgement and to have the clarity to accept the sad and difficult truth, which is that each of us has played

189

a role in the hurts and betrayals that have come our way. This is the path of courage and deep humility, of letting our own false perfection slip away to reveal the hidden self.

Authors Note

I wish to make the point at this juncture to indicate that I am not talking about the terrible abuse and cruelty that is perpetrated against innocent people, but of the everyday hurts that many of us encounter during an average lifetime. It takes a new approach to acknowledge our role in these hurts and conflicts.

The Knight and the Sword

In this journey inwards is to be found the archetype of the questing knight with his sword of truth, setting out to slay the dragons and demons of illusion. This is where we, as questers for honesty, beauty and integrity, begin to see the truth, and for many of us, it can be extremely difficult and painful territory to walk through with grace. 'My perceptions are wrong' is a hard admission, and even harder to admit this to other people, much easier to see them as wronging us. However, this false perception places us in the powerless realm of becoming a victim, which in itself brings mountains of difficulties. The sword of clarity and truth is the sword of refined inner perception, coupled with the grace and balance of seeing our own flaws as treasures of learning.

The grace of metal therefore helps in the separation of the rights from the wrongs inside the mind. The virtue of metal is courage. This is not the courage to slay other people, but the courage to slay the darkness within ourselves that now only hinders the progress of the awakening soul. Consider the archetype of St George and the Dragon. St George had the courage and power to slay the dragon with his sword, which is a metaphor for where we must all arrive at some time in the progress of the soul journey and is analogous to slaying the internal demons of deceit that do not serve the light of internal awakening. There are many stories that convey this level of human development both in religious texts, myths and fairy tales. This is the realm of the battleground between light and dark as herald to the stark choices that the element of metal offers.

Affirmation to Awaken the Courage of Metal

I am truth.
I am precious and valuable.
I am clear and strong and stand in my own light of truth.
I have the courage to make healthy choices
in my thoughts
and in my attitudes.
I breathe in the light of inspiration to illumine my path.

When the light of truth shines brightly, lies and untruths are revealed. This is not to say that all that is dark or hidden is somehow bad or evil. Dark can be soft and loving and mysterious, holding unrevealed and unrealised potential. As treasure waiting to be discovered. The po spirits operate within the forces of opposites, yin and yang, to hold perfect balance and harmony.

Instinct for What is Right – the Wild Animal Nature

The spirit of metal is the spirit of the pure and just that meets out fairness. It is the deeper instinct for what is right and what is wrong. We always know when our internal voice, the instinct has been overridden, more often than not it becomes rationalised by the mind or compromised by a weakness of will or a distorted kindness. We tell ourselves stories about why we're following the mind in favour of a deeper instinct. 'Oh, just this once, she'll realise that she's pushed me too far next time' we say as a friend makes another unreasonable demand. The instinct screams 'don't do it', and the energy drops leaving you drained and empty. But the friend doesn't realise, and your self-respect plummets again.

Your instinct is your wild animal nature and is the power of your immune response. It is in place as a friend and guardian, always protecting your best interests. Every time the instinct is overridden, ignored or betrayed, the boundaries of the immune system are compromised. A good strong boundary of self-respect and respect for other people helps to create a strong immune system.

The qi of protection calls you to break down battlements and fortresses of defence and to have in place strong and flexible boundaries that can move and change with the autonomy of your own growth. To be well protected does not mean to be harsh, but rather to know where you stand within your own self as truth. Many people with weak boundaries try to encompass everything and everyone. They see everyone's points of view and defer to the next idea that comes along or the next person's view that is stronger than their own.

It is wonderful to expand and to encompass and to change and grow, but only when you know where you stand, and come from a strong centre of self-respect and honour. To respect yourself is to offer healthy respect to others and the honouring of self and others is a potent teaching of the metal element.

A Vow

Take some quiet and uninterrupted time.
Breathe quietly in and out allowing your breath to settle into its own rhythm.
Visualise pure white light.
Imagine it filling your lungs as you breathe in.
Gently allow the whole of your body to fill with this light.
Imagine it flowing outwards beyond the confines of your physical being.
Relax into the flow of light.
Gently bring to mind the times and the circumstances in which you dishonour yourself.
Make no judgements, just allow thoughts and memories to surface from the deep and the hidden.
See the rocks and boulders moving away as light flows in.
Keep breathing and keep flowing light.
Gently forgive yourself for the acts of dishonour.
Gently forgive the other people who you thought were responsible.

Make a vow;
'From this moment I deeply honour myself and invoke the courage to hold fast
to this vow.'

White is the healing colour of metal and is associated with purification and clarity. When the light of truth or realisation shines into situations and relationships, the view can appear very different, and often the need to blame other people and to defend your own position just fades away. These are the 'Aha' moments of awareness when the part that we have played in our own betrayal, hurt or persecution is realised. Once these realisations emerge into the conscious mind, then they are no longer part of the rocks and boulders of the hidden self. This is the light of truth and is the light that purifies. It is so powerful that it has the capacity to release swathes of darkness with incoming realisations of truth.

The Power of Words

The Metal element is the breath of life, giving rise to the power of speech and the creative expression of our deeper self. That which is created and vocalised in the outer world is reflected from the inner world. Words have immense power, creating the resonance of manifestation. We are told in the story of creation that 'In the beginning was the word.' Creation began with a sound and the waves that emanated from the sound had immense power. There is some tricky territory in the awakening of the higher realms of this element that is known as 'speaking my truth'. This arises with an awakening of self-respect and in the right situations can be healing and cathartic, particularly for those people who have felt so compressed and repressed that they have been unable to use the power of their own voice and reason. How wonderful and liberating to encompass new life and to be able to vocalise.

This can mark a profound turning point and be a time of celebration and renewal.

However, there are others who feel entitled and justified in 'speaking their truth' anywhere and everywhere, and this can be inappropriate and potentially hurtful and damaging to others, as the self demands to be heard regardless. Beware the voice that rings out like a clanging bell, be careful to examine the motive that underlies it.

Awakening into the Level of Higher Consciousness

The Corporeal Soul

On the other side of the power of speech, resides the power of listening. Listening is an art of grace. Listening involves quietening down your own noisy internal world and opening yourself to someone else. The ability to truly listen is one of the higher realms of the Metal element, and it is perhaps now more appropriate to use the softer term 'air' as we approach the more rarefied realms of soul. As you listen to your own breath, so you can begin to open outwards like a beautiful flower to other people, listening to their rhythm and their breath of life.

True listening involves all the senses and means putting yourself to one side as an act of selfless service. With selflessness comes the grace of courage as to become of true service, you may be asked to go beyond your known self and enter unknown territory. How far are you willing to go in service of God? Do you have the courage to hold sacred ground for your own evolution and to have respect and honour for other people's ways and for their sacred ground? The aspect that connects us in this element is the quest for truth and realisation of self as a soul of light. We all breathe air, and in this breathing, we are connected.

Listen

Take some time out from this busy and noisy world as a gift for your soul.
Take some precious time to be quiet, to be still, and a whole new world will gradually unfold.
Please take some time to listen
Gently sink your attention inside, seeking the quiet and the stillness.
Allow nothing to intrude.

Here is your holy ground, your sacred space.

Listen to the words of your soul as they arise within the silence.

Becoming Courage

It takes courage to become truly truthful. No exaggeration, no embellishment, hiding or twisting away. It takes courage to cut away untruth and illusion and to stand and live within the pure light of soul. The way of air asks, "How do I act out of my own truth without betrayal?" Betrayals and untruths can arise in the smallest and most subtle of ways, in everyday interactions and everyday choices. Over time, these subtleties build into a structure that impacts on life. At the level of soul, the truth is always offered through a loving heart and never as a harshness either to self or others.

Through this element, the soul matures in its journey of light, becoming purified and refined through experience, through the grief of loss and through the inspiration of heavenly forces. The animal-like instinct of the lower spheres is replaced with the purity of service to the divine. As the self is dedicated in service to God and to life, it takes on a new and higher resonance, serving a force higher than the everyday self. Lower emotions and motivations fall away, and the person feels and responds differently. It is as though re-shaped, re-modelled, re-born, and life takes on a finer, softer and lighter texture as the old and outworn self gradually dies away. The presence of soul radiates and the whole person is lit by an unseen and radiant light.

We have reached the realm of the holy, of the sacred and most spiritual. It is from here that clear guidance directs the life, and the feeling is of following something higher, rather than of creating from the self. This is true inspiration and the task of the person is to remain open and clear enough to sustain this level of being. This is the space beyond the mundane, beyond the everyday. It is the sacred, dwelling place of all that is pure, beautiful and true.

The Realm of Divinity

Learn to breathe and you will have life
Learn to breathe well and you will have good health
Learn to breathe deeply and you will live long
Learn to breathe inwardly and you will awaken your soul
As you awaken your soul and breathe into the connectedness of all things
Here you will find the depth of peace… your homecoming.

Chapter 6

The Zhi Spirit of Water

Attunement Meditation

The Wisdom Spirit of Winter

Here you are at the Source of the great flowing river of your own life.
Pause for a while before you step in. Pause to reflect and look around you.
All is shimmering with an iridescence that comes from the deep.
And gazing, you see gleaming before you, the great mystery, the mystery of creation.
The magic, the possibilities… all are here, and you cannot tell what is real and what reflected… in this moment all is the same, and all is revealed as one in this beautiful shimmering light.
Aligned with the will of heaven.
The flowing river of the Tao lies before you, strong and silently it moves.
Gathering of your will, you step in.
Step into the eddies and the flows of all that has been and all that will be. The flows of your soul life, your past revisited for healing and balance and your future revealed in the beauty of your soul light. Will you reach for the past, for the present, the future?
Ah, all is here blended in the light of soul.

Your loving, your letting, your fears and your leaving, your feeling and the wisdom of your deeper learning.

All is here, all is communicated through the ebbs and flows, illuminated by divine light.

Thus, a beginning is an ending, and an ending a beginning, where to start and where to end… all streams on and on and on, and the rivers flow, the oceans roar, and the tiny drops of dew sparkle with an iridescence so pure…

There you stand amongst the shimmering, the glimmering, the gleaming, the sheening.

Long before distortion, deviation or diversion, all is as it should be… it could be… it can be…

Tiny fragments of light float and flow around you, within you, dipping and diving, disappearing into vaporous clouding, spiriting, lifting drifting flying heavenward, dipping earthward.

The sweet calling of soul guides the way.

The Zhi Spirit of the Water Element

Spirit of Potential and Change

Winter is the lowest point of the yearly cycle of the seasons, when temperatures and light sinks and life slows down and moves within the hidden mysterious depths. The Will for Life is strong and magnetic, attracting creative forces, and winter presents a vital phase in the journey of wisdom for the individual soul. Winter takes us into the dark and cold, so that the hidden may be uncovered, and potentially claimed. The zhi is the spirit of the ancestral line, of karmic rebalancing and of connecting the past with the present and the future as a continuum of life. The will of heaven flows down to earth through the zhi, aligning with the will of the individual soul. It teaches that to swim against the tides is to create difficulties, but to embrace the flow is to travel with ease along the Tao river of life.

Can you follow your own riverways towards your highest destiny?

The Essence of Water Power

The essence of power of the water element is to swim, move and change with the tides of life. Yours is the power to surge through to your heights and depths and emerge chameleon-like in your ability to change and adapt as circumstances require. Yours is the power to see the potent reflections of life, and to dive deeply into the mysterious unknown.

The Harmonious
Resonance of Water

Season is winter.

Colour is blue or black.

Sound is of the droning of the waves as they come and go.

Aroma is fresh as newly fallen rain or putrid as stagnant water.

In the body, the water element governs the fluid levels in the body, the bladder and kidneys, adrenals and nervous system, bones and marrow, brain, hormonal system, the ears and the ability to listen.

The qualities invoked by water are both gentleness and a strength of will. Intelligence, introspection, supportive, self-reliant, adaptable, changeable, charismatic and magnetic, psychic, reflective.

The Disharmonious
Resonance of Water

Lack of will in many forms, nervous and paranoid, unreliable, overly driven, overly dramatic Dark dreams and thoughts. Fear in many arenas in life, or lack of fear when to be fearful is an appropriate response.

Symptoms – Conditions affecting the bladder and kidneys, such as cystitis, incontinence. Low back pain. Back problems and conditions of the spine. Nervous complaints – anxiety, insomnia, and more severe conditions of the brain and nervous system such as paranoid schizophrenia, bipolar, attention deficit disorder. Hormonal and developmental disorders.

Awakening into Higher Consciousness

Karma and Beyond...

The wisdom to align your personal will with the will of heaven and follow the course of the great river of life. By aligning your will, you are able to heal the karma that is yours to heal as you can see your own journey reflected in the deeper wisdom paths of your life.

Song of the Water Element

Pause for a moment.

Listen.

Listen to the tides of life flowing through your body.

Listen to the thoughts flowing through your head.

Listen to your feelings as they rise and fall like tidal waves.

Listen to the sounds in your outside world.

This moment holds all your life in a sacred vessel.

Here is the magic,

The coming together, the confluence of

All that you have been

and

All that you will be.

Be still, listening deeply into the wisdom power of the quiet and the still.

Winter
Season of Water

The phase of the Water element shows its face most keenly in winter.

Welcome to the watery world of winter – phase of subtle beauty and starkly frozen contrasts. Winter is the natural phase of hibernation, drawing on the deeper reserves laid down in earlier months of light, warmth and plenty. The days are short, and nights seem eternal. Many people have an instinctive dislike and even a fear of the dark, longing for lighter, warmer and more optimistic times. In contrast, there are those who love these quieter times, as a refuge from the stresses and strains of an overly busy lifestyle and make use of this phase to press the pause button.

There is an intensity as temperatures fall. Icy air seers into the senses and chills us down to the bones. Time seems to drag with the diminishing natural forces. We huddle against the cold, natural energy slowing and diminishing. What could be better than curling up in front of a roaring fire with a bowl of hot soup? The spirit of winter speaks of survival, and the will to care for the mind, body and spirit during times of lack.

The countryside is laid bare and pointed-fingered branches lie in stark relief across a bleak horizon. Nothing is now hidden from view by lush foliage or by rippling crops in fields. The once lush landscape now pared down to its bare minimum. Winter horizons seem vast and unbroken in their bleakness, while each unique six-pointed filigree snowflake delights the senses and focuses the mind on the miraculous. The landscape disappears like magic, blanketed in pure white snow, transformed as though by the hand of a magician. Sharp talons of icicles lace the windowsills and individual crystals of snow glisten in sunlight, transforming even the most ordinary surroundings into the extraordinary. So too with mist, with rains and floods. They can all transform the landscape in an instant, and it is in these moments that we realise the power of water and the fear that arises in us if our survival is threatened.

In the unfurling of the year, winter, particularly, is an acute reminder of the seasonal cycles, being stark and uncompromising in making its presence felt. Sometimes cold, sharp, well-defined, it arrives abruptly on the tail of autumn, and sometimes it arrives floundering in clouds of perpetual grey. In whatever way it makes its entrance, it cannot be ignored and urges us to adjust to this phase of slowing down and adapting to diminishing light and falling temperatures.

With winter comes a vital phase in the dance of life. It is the lowest point in the cycle of qi and a reminder that after the life and abundance of spring and summer come the seasons of death and rebirth. When nothing is visible on the surface, forces of nature are very much at play, activating and bringing forwards new growth for the future year. Deep within the silent and the hidden, new life is powerfully and quietly forming.

The water element is both guide and teacher through the dark and harsh months of winter. Winter is the point of deepest yin in the yearly cycle, where qi is at its lowest ebb and cannot sink any further. It holds the mystery of life itself and the wondrous potential for new life deep within its hidden places. As the natural forces of winter open the pathway to this hidden and mysterious realm, the perfect opportunity arises in us to mirror this movement of qi, and to sink deeply within our own self.

How the Water Element Arises in the Body?

In the body, the bony structures, including the teeth, are governed by water. Just as winter takes the landscape back to its 'bare bones' providing the structures upon which the new season's growth can flourish, so in people, the skeleton forms the structure around which the health and movement of the body is created, and also forms a system of support for the vulnerable internal organs. The ears are the orifice governed by water, and the sense is hearing. The ability to truly listen requires the listener to become still and receptive, both of which are qualities of water.

Water underpins our very existence and forms the deepest essence upon which the individual is established. This personal essence is inherited through genetic structures of the ancestral line and also carries the unfoldment of the soul's learning and growing wisdom, which in some traditions is called karma. The Water element governs the rhythms of change, in particular the hormonal changes that forge the growth and development from child to adult. These important cycles are said to happen every seven years for men, and every eight years for women. These pivotal times are the time of birth, the loss of the first teeth around 7 or 8 years old, puberty, the age of procreation, the age of maturation, menopause, followed by the gateway into wisdom and older years, and finally into death and the mysterious beyond.

People with a propensity towards water in their elemental makeup display this element through the language arising from their body. There may be a translucence to the complexion or perhaps a bluey tinge around the features, mirroring a wintery sky. The voice has a droning quality echoing the relentless streaming of water through the landscape, or it may alternately gush and then retreat, like the waves upon the shore, or a bubbling mountain spring. The person may appear to be still, but nervous movement can be seen in a tapping finger or the swing of a foot or a nervous 'tick'. Conversely, they may be forever on the move, but a stillness can be detected deep within. Movement and stillness are keynotes for the Water element. An aroma, which is described in Chinese medicine as putrid, arises from the body, smelling like rainwater or a still lake. It occasionally arises as an 'ozone' smell like the sea, or a smell of general 'dampness'.

The kidneys and bladder are the major organs of water. The kidneys have the function of filtering, stabilising and purifying water in the body and, of course, need a plentiful supply of fresh drinking water to keep them healthy and functioning well. The kidney meridian arises in the soles of the feet at a point called 'Bubbling Spring'. This is a point of joyful renewal, rebirth and celebration of life itself. The meridian circulates around the inner ankles, surging up the inside of the legs and powerfully up the front of the body into the chest. The points on the chest are of particular interest as they are in the region of the heart. Where the Water element meets the Fire element of the heart, deep spiritual transformations are possible, and it is these spirit points that allow access to the healing of a person's spirit. In my own practice, the treatment of these points has had a rapid and positive effect on my patients at times when they have felt particularly lost or low, or somehow disconnected from their own lives.

There is a point called 'Spirit Burial Ground', which can help to revive a person from the burial grounds of their own despair, calling them back to the vitality of their own life. The very first time I used this point in treatment, my patient arose from the couch, declaring that she felt as though she could start again with her life. She left looking bright, relaxed and refreshed.

It can be very helpful to tap or to gently palpate this point at those times when you are feeling buried or lost in your own life. Kidney 24, or Spirit Burial Ground, is to be found in the chest, between the third and fourth ribs, around three finger widths from the centre of the sternum. There is one each side of the chest, and they can feel tender to the touch. Use one or two fingers to gently massage or tap both sides at the same time, releasing your qi with an affirmation such as this one.

> I release myself from fear and constriction,
> rising to meet life
> through my fullest potential.

The other organ of water, the bladder, is concerned with the balance of fluids and the elimination of impurities from the body. The bladder meridian is the longest meridian in the body, signifying the vital role of water. It surges from the inner corner of the eyes, up over the head, down the neck and spine and down the back of the legs ending along the outside edge of the feet at the furthest tip of the little toe. There is a double bladder channel running down either side of the spine indicating its importance in maintaining the health, strength and fluidity of the back, spine and nervous system.

The back is a vital support, both physically and emotionally, and holds the strength of the will. Situated along the bladder meridian are important access points for all major organs and functions, indicating the importance of the water phase of qi as master communicator in the treatment of the whole person.

The element of water spans the journey through the past and future, bringing us to the exalted moment of living and being in the present, the connecting point between what was, and what will be. As the power of the bladder qi is to do with the power of surging towards the future, so the kidney qi is to do with connection and communication with the past.

The Wisdom Way of Reflection

Take some quiet time for reflection.
Imagine dropping all connections with your past, your future, your fears and
your daily concerns.
Allow yourself the space to move towards a magical stillness, taking your time
and feeling your way.
Feel the beauty and power of being with yourself in the presence of this silent
moment.
All that you have been
and
All that you may be
is captured and encapsulated here and now
in this time and this space.

The Zhi Spirits of Water

Can you surge to the depths and heights of your
highest potential?

Although a groan often goes up when it rains, life needs water for its very
existence. The surface of this planet is largely water, with rains replenishing what

is lost through vapourisation in a cycle of rising and falling. Water is everywhere. The atmosphere holds water vapour, and water is retained in vast snow fields and glaciers. Rivers, rain, seas, lakes, mists and early morning dew are all sources of this life-giving element.

We too are largely water. Human babies grow and develop in a watery world. Water is so essential to life that although in temperate regions of the world it is taken for granted, but in dryer areas, it was traditionally hailed and revered as a life-giving deity, and ceremonies and thanksgiving were dedicated to its presence and to the invocation of rain. The life that we know and recognise completely depends on water.

The zhi are the spirits of the Water element and support the phase of winter, teaching the power of stillness and reflection as a path to the wisdom of self-knowledge. They are the spirits of potential, whose task is to help in the evolution of new ideas, new potential and new choices. To sink deeply is to discover hidden depths, and many of us resonate with this phase as a time for retreat, discovery and reflection. Other people may not have this resonance within their nature and may instead mirror the more difficult side of the descent into winter, feeling depressed, lonely, gloomy and lacking in energy as light and natural forces slip away.

Winter offers a change of pace, as support for the incoming zhi, and creates space and opportunity for the re-building of inner reserves that may have become diminished through too much activity. It's vital to take a step back for a while to recoup what has been lost during more naturally active times of year, otherwise, like rivers that have become dry, your reserves run the risk of never being replenished and health runs the risk of becoming compromised. Once the deeper inner reserves, which Chinese medicine likens to underground rivers, are depleted, it can take time and care to rebuild them. Quiet and restorative pursuits such as reading, walking, yoga, Tai chi and meditation can help to replenish these vital reserves over time.

The nature of the spirits of water is to change, to reflect and to purify. The Water element with its teasing changeability almost dares you to begin the journey inwards. It invites you to a deeper knowing of who you are and encourages the opening to the mystery of your soul life. The zhi bring mystery and magic and, if you are willing, can take you down into the terror of the dark, of the unfamiliar, the as yet unknown.

Water is infinite in its fluidity, having no form of its own, but reshapes and changes according to external conditions. It is the shapeshifter, the infinite changer. Water compels you to go deeper and carries you into the depths and darkness of the shadowy, elusive world of feelings and emotions.

Listen to the deep world within yourself,
Your changeable nature.
Your willingness
Your fluidity

Like trying to hold water with your fingers, emotions too can be difficult to grasp on to – changeable, dangerous, powerful. Like water, they can ebb and flow to reflect both stillness and peaceful time and the stormy pummelling tides of life. The currents of your own life will carry you to wherever healing needs to take place. What may be called karma is the unhealed and unresolved which lies ready to be integrated, settled, healed and ultimately made peace with.

Water by its very nature is the communicator.

The zhi spirits teach of communication, both on a personal level or a more expanded level. Communication, like water, is vital to our survival, particularly in this modern technological world. In addition to technology, it governs any other form of communication such as the road and rail networks, flight paths and canal systems. It also oversees our internal communication networks of the nervous system which receive, interpret and transmit signals and responses, systems of transportation of blood and fluids and the meridian system.

The Spirit of Water as Reflection

Contrast and paradox are the keynotes of water. People with a water archetype can be dramatic, exaggerated, charismatic, changeable, at times introverted, at times extroverted. They want to hide, and they want to be visible, all is contrast, making them tricky and elusive, difficult to predict. They can be 'cool' in temperament or a gushing wave of emotion – who knows? My son described himself as a 'noisy quiet person', and perhaps this best summarises the forces at play, which can encompass and hold the extremes of life.

There are depths of soul at work in these internal landscapes, giving these people a magical and charismatic quality. They can be magnetic and charming, but 'expect the unexpected' is their motto, as they change and flow with their own deep impulses. Survival is the drive that galvanises them. They can be strong-willed and ambitious with something of the pioneer about them as they 'live on the edge' and like to forge their own path in life. They can be strong-willed, laughing in the face of their deeper fears, and can be very reliable in an everyday sense, with their ability to 'just keep going'. They are often good during crisis as their strong will enables them to stay afloat in difficult situations. Paramedics, mountain and sea rescuers, the explorers and inventors, technological wizards, mystics and magicians, and those people who can overcome themselves and go more deeply and beyond the everyday are under the auspices of water.

Fear – Emotion of Water

Fear stands at the very threshold of life and death.
Fear is stark and dramatic and will hold you in
talons of ice.

Just as water can encourage the free and pioneering spirit, at the other end of the spectrum resides the challenge of the deep and dark emotional self. The Water element, as the keeper of the nervous system and keeper of the mystery of dark and hidden depths, lives with nervousness and fear as its emotion. Fear is the response to threat. Whether real or imagined, the response is the same, activating internal chemical reactions to fight or flight, and occasionally at times of heightened fear, a person may 'freeze'. The zhi spirits of water teach of authentic responses, and hold up a mirror of authenticity, asking, "Is this level of fear necessary or appropriate?" It can be easy to sink beneath the waves, feeling overwhelmed by whirlpools of emotions and to view all life events and calls for change as 'life-threatening'. However, to be overly dramatic in reaction is to diminish and exhaust the spirits of the zhi and to place undue strain upon your vital organs.

Emotions are like water – powerful, all consuming, overwhelming. They can whip you up into a whirlpool and can drag you down in a powerful undercurrent. They are creative, they are destructive. They are ugly, they are beautiful. They can flip and change in an instant, taking you through a waterwheel of ups and down. You can drown in emotion. They are the greatest teachers about you as an individual. They hold up a valuable mirror to you to show you react and respond to life. Much emotion is reactive and has the demon fear behind it. Fear is the language of the lower forces of the water element, and if unrecognised, it can dominate your power of choice. Fear prevents everything and that is its nature. Fear stops you in your tracks. Fear tells you not to do this and not to do that. Fear is eroding to the life of the soul. Fear is a tricky, manipulative demon and can hide in the dark recesses of your hidden and unknown self.

Finding Your Way Through Fear

Sit quietly in an undisturbed space and give yourself a little time.
Mentally bring to mind something in your life that invokes fear and gently acknowledge how you feel in this moment.
Notice how your body feels physically.
The high and jumping beating of your heart.
The tightness of your shallow breathing.
The watery aching in your back and stiffness in your joints.
The incessant pulse in your temples.
The dread in the pit of your stomach.
Give space to all these sensations and more, as they surge and push their way through your body.
This is real.
This is how you are reacting to the event or events that you are facing and this is how you feel.
Take a breath in, hold it for a moment or two and breathe out with a deep sigh.

Then turn and face your fear.

Face that fear lurking inside you that has brought you to this point.

Name your fear aloud. 'I am fearful of…'

Find some description and some detail – how does it look to you?

How does this fear affect your life?

Does it have a colour, a form?

Visualise that colour or that form leaving your body and leaving your life.

Feel the feeling of freedom, allowing these new sensations to flow through you.

Take in the detail of these new sensations

To make friends with fear, or in other words to become deeply familiar with it and treat it lightly, is to call back your power from the depths of yourself.

To face it is to free yourself.

Freedom is the greatest gift that you can give to yourself.

Fear also has a protective and side and can be a very helpful in preventing you from putting yourself or others into dangerous or ill-advised situations. Fear can stop you from taking unwise risks. It can prove to be both best friend and worst enemy and calls you to understand its ways and workings and how it plays out in your own life.

Make fear your friend and ally.

Water Element as Philosopher

The water element arises through the nervous system and brain. The spirit of water is related to the intelligence that develops through actively seeking knowledge and from experience gained through navigating the many waterways of life. The quest for knowledge and wisdom, and the fulfilment of destiny, is guided by the zhi, which resonate with a sense of destiny and the journey of the emerging wisdom of the soul. The water element can awaken the high intellect, emerging as the 'Absent-Minded Professor' archetype, pioneering and absorbed in the quest for knowledge above all else, but untidy and impractical, the dreary mundanities of life becoming submerged beneath oceans of learning.

The zhi oversee the power of your beliefs. Your beliefs underpin your experience of life in the same way that water underpins the existence of life itself. What you believe changes everything. The life that unfolds is a reflection of deep beliefs that lie within. If you believe that the world will end tomorrow, will you live differently to how you would live if you believed you could live forever? If you believe someone hates you, will your behaviour be different to how it would be if you believe that this same someone loves you? If you believe in God, are your attitudes different to those who do not believe in God? If you believe in a vengeful and judgemental deity, do you behave differently to how you would under the care of a forgiving and loving one?

Beliefs hold one nation in conflict with another and one person in conflict with another. Beliefs can create hatred and wars. Humanity seems to seek 'sameness' to feel safe. Differences in beliefs, religion, deities, cultures and way of life can appear as threatening and give space to our friend Mr Fear Demon. He prowls around at the level of survival and likes us to feel 'safe' no matter what. Do you feel threated by trying something different, or by the unknown, or by other people who hold different beliefs or ideals than your own?

The beliefs that you hold as sacred are the directing force of your life. If things aren't working too well, and your life is beset by difficulties, disappointments or unrealised dreams, then it may be the right time to delve deeply into your beliefs. Water holds the Archetype of Philosopher, and it may be time to consider your own philosophy of life.

The philosophy of Taoism is the way of nature. Chinese wisdom likened the journey through life to a flowing river, understanding that, at times, we are carried by the tides and, at times, we exhaust ourselves in an effort to swim against them. To follow the currents of this great river, which is called the Tao, with its cycles and rhythms is known as following the Tao, or The Way or The Way of Wisdom, or the Path of the Soul. There are many terms and philosophies that seek to interpret this with words and language. The Tao asks that you to embrace and flow with change to reflect your own changing and expanding cycles of learning and knowledge. It is through a fear of losing our own free will, that we very often place ourselves in direct opposition to the laws of change, forgetting that change is at the heart of progress, evolution and development.

To be fluid and adaptable can be great attributes when following the tides of life. However, we can be creatures of habit, erecting walls of resistance, preferring our own 'free will' over the will of heaven. The way of the soul is to blend the will of heaven with your own free will, not being resistant to either, but flowing appropriately with the wisdom needed to know when to direct and when to follow.

As you become more deeply immersed within the mystery of life
Fear releases its hold
and
The will of the soul becomes a deep reflection of the will of heaven

The Water Element out of Balance

When Fear Stops the Flow

Above all the other elements, water can reflect the stark reality of life. As you gaze within a still and serene lake, you see the surroundings, trees, sky, clouds, perfectly reflected. They both appear 'real', but one is merely the reflection of the other, giving rise to the questions, 'What is real and what is illusion?' Is the life that we lead 'real' or merely a reflection of our beliefs and attitudes?

People who experience an imbalance in their element of water often have difficulty in knowing what is real and what is fantasy. Fear and other powerful emotional states can take hold and lead the imagination into a whirling pool of imagined drama. Dreams can be vivid and unnerving, and sleep can be erratic and easily disturbed. Attention span can come and go in short bursts. It is impossible for the nervous system to be still.

When your still and serene internal lake becomes compromised through the pollution of unwanted thoughts or through trauma and fear, reality can become overwhelmed by waves and whirlpools of illusion. There can be a point where you no longer recognise what is real or unreal, truth or illusion, which can lead to eddies and currents of lies, deceit, betrayal. 'The truth is enough' is a strong maxim to live by. As the internal waters settle and clear, so the mind finds balance and the way of truth becomes revealed and reflected back to your through your experience of life.

There are people who love to see the 'worst' in a situation perhaps because it offers more scope for the dramatic than the 'real'. Water loves the 'dramatic', so, who gives a hoot about what is rational or 'real'? Water people love to cause a stir by embellishing the truth and also love the 'horror' of creating worst case scenarios. "Let's go for high drama, it's much more exciting!" cries unbalanced water. I once asked a very bright and intelligent lady (my lovely mother) with this propensity, whether any of the things that she feared had ever happened or come true? "Oh no," she said. "It's just how I am!" She thought that the 'real was boring' and wanted more drama and intensity.

Still Your Inner Waters

Take time to be still in a peaceful place.
Allow your mind to weave its way towards tranquillity and your senses to open
to your surroundings.
Breathe slowly and deeply into the magical moment,
Allowing illusion to fall from you like
Stones falling to the bottom of a still lake

There is a side to water which is relentless, it goes on and on regardless. People with this imbalance in their energetic makeup can be the ones who talk endlessly, monopolising all conversation, often with the embellishment of dramatics, as they like to keep the attention of their audience and are terrified of being rejected. Water can be tedious, it can be intensely boring – drip, drip, drip. On it goes until even the most stalwart amongst us becomes eroded.

The voice drones on like a pounding ocean and can be heard beneath and beyond other voices. It appears that their watery nature is fearful of ever stopping – what might happen? Might I die? Cease to exist? How terrifying… This overly 'driven' quality can spill and splash into work and leisure time; they never seem to be able to stop, everything flowing seamlessly into the next thing, and then the next. This quality can lead to people being highly effective, but the flip side of this coin is that this way of life is extremely tiring.

Unbalanced water can emerge as a nerviness and jumpiness that can be provoked by even the most mundane and everyday event such as the ringing of a phone or the slam of a door. The adrenaline is surging, propelling the person to take flight or to fight. There is a tremulous quality to these people, and they may have the appearance of being insubstantial, transparent – ready to vanish before your eyes!

They can sometimes appear aloof and uncaring, but this can often be the result of their level of immersion in the task at hand, or in their inner world of thoughts and intrigue, which makes them self-absorbed. There is something enigmatic and hidden, as though they are holding a secret, or part of them is hidden away. This can be the case, as an aspect of the Water element likes to hide in cracks and crevices, underground and in hidden spaces. It can prove difficult to really know these people, who are very good at hiding by reflecting and mirroring the people around them. This earns them their shapeshifting quality, as they can appear to change before your eyes according to either their internal or external environments.

Another face of water out of balance can be seen revealed in the person who is overly conscious of other people, overly driven to keep going to meet all and every demand and often trying to fill the gaps left by less conscientious people. These people can have a level of psychic awareness, reflecting the moods and emotions around them. They can 'mop up' or 'absorb' negativity, which leaves them feeling drained and washed out. Beware those folks who like to latch on and 'drain' you – the psychic vampires. If you feel drained and depleted around certain people, it's important to re-establish a strong sense of self, and if this is impossible in their presence, it may be a good idea to avoid too much contact until you are more established in your own presence and your own riverways. It's important not to get swept into the undercurrents of negativity.

Water Contemplation for Establishing
Your Own Sense of Self

Take some quiet time to reflect upon your own natural rhythms.
The gentle beating of your heart, your breath coming and going.
Have some awareness of the sensations, fluids and movements flowing through
your body.
Become aware of the skin that protects your beautiful body, the structures that
give you form
and of the space around and within you in which you move and live.
Allow your whole being to settle into the familiar frame of your own self and
your own tides and rhythms.
If you have absorbed some negativity, or feel 'not yourself', then try the
following meditation. The following meditation will help to purify and cleanse
your energy.

Meditation for Cleansing
and Purification
Through Water

Take a little time to establish yourself as described above.
Now imagine that you are making your way to a beautiful lake.
The sun is high in the sky, and nature looks her beautiful and colourful best.
The sky is endlessly blue, and the path upon which you tread is clear and easy.
You arrive at the lake, perfect and tranquil.
You stand upon the shore and look at the calm and still water glinting and
sparkling in the sunlight.
The surroundings are perfectly reflected and mirrored in the clear water.
You step in and the water is soft, warm and gentle surrounding you with its
buoyancy, lifting and carrying you…
As you swim towards the centre, your splashes make rainbows in the sparkling
sunlight. So colourful.
You roll onto you back, feeling held and rocked by the strength of the water
beneath you. You are so relaxed that all the cares, worries and fears that have

undermined your happiness seem to wash away into the water, falling from you like boulders to the bottom of the lake.

You feel lighter and fresher than you have felt for a long time.

The water cleanses you, purifying and refreshing every cell in your being.

When you are ready, make your way to the shore.

You step out of the lake knowing that you are fresh and renewed and ready to return to your everyday life.

Moving into the Shadowlands of the Water Element

Diving into the Hidden and Unknown to Release Yourself

Entering the shadowlands of water, feelings of fear, terror, the horrors of the as yet unborn and unknown, unseen self, hidden and secret are encountered. Here the waters are dark and stagnant, holding negativity in a bottomless void. The silence is brooding like a scene from a horror movie. Terror awaits you. Here lurk all the demons of fear, waiting. Waiting to be fed with the next surge of adrenaline, the next flow of anxious, fearful and unverifiable thoughts and emotions, they lurk in the dark waters.

This is the realm of dark magic, of curses and the dark mythology of folk law. Here is the witchcraft and the dark spells, the fear of evil, the fear that unseen forces can negatively influence your life, the fear that you are somehow separated out and cursed to live in darkness. Reflected in the murky water are the false dreams, the fantasies, the illusions, the deceptions and shady secrets. Making your way through the dark waters, you see the reflections of your own unrealised potential, of opportunities missed and of the life that you could have lived, had fear not walked at your heels.

You come now to a frozen landscape where nothing moves, and all is waiting, stopped in its tracks. Here you find the Sleeping Beauty of your own unrealised self – beautiful, frozen, waiting. Waiting to be freed by the handsome

Prince of your Spirit, whose love melts away the never-ending icy sleep of forgotten potential.

Here, in this phase of energy lies shame. Shame is insidious, creeping and seeping water-like through cracks and crevices. Shame undermines the deeper self and can seriously impact the health. People who carry shame cannot thrive but lie frozen and as dormant as the Sleeping Beauty, waiting to be awakened by the spirit of approval and acceptance. The energetic of chronic shame can erode the deep systems of nerves and hormones, compromising essential reserves of qi needed to fulfil your greater potential. Shame lurks in the shadowlands as a 'life stealer'. You can never appease it enough for it to free you, so you must free yourself. Shame is a distortion of self-worth and is a by-product that can emerge from feeling deeply undermined and not 'enough'.

The wisdom of water teaches that there is always enough and that you as a reflection of the creative forces that have brought you into this life, to the here and now, are enough.

I Am Enough.
I am here to fulfil the journey of my own soul,
through the emerging flows of my life.

Allow these words to gently find their way and sink deeply into your mind, your body and your emotional core. Allow them to erode the last fragments of your shame and to awaken you towards the possibility of a new will for life.

The shadowlands of the Water element are particularly difficult to navigate as they not only appear real to the imagination (and perhaps they are), but they are supported by cultural mythology – fear of hell and damnation, and of hideous demons and unnameable creatures. Just as the realms of light are created from love, the realms of darkness are created from fear. Everyone has the potential to slip within these realms and this is part of the free will of being human. The difficulties arise when you allow yourself to reside here, and to create a reality around these perceptions, without understanding that there is more. With the realisation that you can go through and beyond, comes the faintest chink of light up ahead and even the faintest notion that perhaps it is possible to release yourself and be free from your own land of shadows can create the impetus to do just that.

From my own experience I know how easy it is to 'freeze' when fear tears into you with its talons of ice. There have been times in my own life when I have been faced with what seemed to be insurmountable personal pain. These are the times when we can freeze, or drown in our own emotions, when everything appears black and the way forward is out of sight. I developed a way out of the darkness, which has always, in some unknown and incredible way, worked for me. I began, in a moment of desperation, to imagine a rope or a bridge of energy which I threw from myself towards the light. At the times when I was unable to see the light, I just imagined it being there. In that moment of crisis or pain, I have no idea how I will move from where I am to somewhere different/better/easier, but I throw my energy rope, which I now know to be my strength of will, anyway.

Over time, things always begin to change, helping me to set my sights on moving through the darkness to somewhere else. I now know that it is essential to imagine moving through and beyond dark and difficult times, even if you are not clear about how to do this, or what lies ahead. It is at these times that the power of the movement of the wood element comes into play. As you will discover later in this book, wood is the element of direction, movement and imagination, and can be exactly what's needed to get us out of a dark hole.

On coming through the darkness, I discover that I have always learnt something more about myself, and this knowledge has, over time, created a strong personal will. Like a strong rope in a torrent, it gives me something to hold onto and, like my imaginary bridge, draws me through adversity. If experience teaches wisdom, then the knowledge that it is possible to change, or move or adjust, creates the will to have a go at whatever it is that you want to achieve.

Water on the Rise

Starting to Flow

Then come the profound and tumultuous realisation that none of this is fixed, and none of it is any more real than the beliefs that you hold, the emotions that compel you, and the thoughts in your head. Beliefs and thoughts will charge the emotional content of your own landscape, creating the droughts, floods and whirlpools of your own responses and reactions.

The zhi spirits of water love nothing more than to move and to flow. They are chameleon-like in their gentle skills at adapting to different territories and conditions, whether of the external landscape or of the internal weather conditions of emotional currents. They 'go with the flow', with a sense of ease that comes with the wisdom of experience. The zhi teach that the way of pleasurable ease is the way of true communication, and so when freed, they flow in endless communication between the higher and lower realms, bringing the will of heaven to awaken and enlighten the shadowlands of fear.

Cold and fear slows everything down, and warmth and love speeds everything up. The zhi spirits bring adaptability, and the love of changing pace and changing frequency, not wanting to become in any way 'stuck'. To become stuck is to become stagnant. Stagnant water is dead and reeking and can no longer support the healthy flows of a creative life. It is deeply unhealthy and internally can give rise to profound health issues, such as exhaustion, premature aging, long-term depression and anxiety, and issues around menstruation and fertility. It can be implicated in painful conditions such as gout, osteoporosis, back pain, and conditions of the bladder and kidneys.

To be willing to become more fluid within your own self is a keynote to rising out of fear. Willingness and the strength of will needed to see it through are the signs of a strong and healthy water element. Be willing with yourself and willing with others but get to know the extent of your flow. A sense of will is the strength of the zhi, and so is the wisdom to know when to be strong willed and to stay with that power, and when to be willing to change and be fluid enough to adapt to different conditions. In my own practice, I have realised with humility that I cannot heal or help my patients by my own force of will. My own will needs to meet the willingness (will) of my patient, and I then align my own will with a higher will if this is what is needed to help my patient towards a higher trajectory of health.

As qi becomes less dense, so this is reflected through to the emotions, which become freer. If previously there was a tendency towards becoming stuck, frozen or log-jammed into a particular emotional arena, then with more fluidity comes an experience of a greater range of feelings and emotions, without the underpinning of fear as its habitual basis. Our culture has quite strict rules about which emotions we are 'supposed' to feel and express, and the British Stiff Upper Lip certainly doesn't inspire the confidence needed to feel at ease with your own emotional self. We are deeply emotional beings and to deny this is to deny the richest and most colourful part of self. The spirits of the zhi encourage emotion to flow freely like beautiful rainbows of energy.

Imagine sunlight catching drops of water and turning them into rainbow prisms. Allow yourself to feel as broadly and expansively as the rainbow's arc. Try not to stay too long with one colour but move freely between them all so that the whole spectrum comes alive within you. Delight in your emotions and let them become expressions of who you are, guarding against becoming frozen into just one. Release your fears of flowing yourself out into the great flow of life. Release the ropes and constrictions that dull your colours and prevent you from being authentic. Come up from the mud that sticks you to the bottom of the river and enjoy the freedom of swimming freely in your own tides.

Try the following when you feel stuck in the riverbed of your own life –

How does this 'stuck' feeling feel inside you?
Can you assign a colour to it?
Gently sit with this feeling and the colour of the feeling, trying to understand how it arises within yourself and your life. Try following this thread of colour backwards through your life to its origins.
It may take you back to a person or an event, or it may seem to stretch back into the unknown.
Imagine changing this thread to a thread of sparkling light.
See it releasing you from the dreariness of your past and setting you free.
Free to discover the delights of floating, and swimming in your own tides of life.

You may now recognise your thread as being fear. Give your thread a colour, a texture and bring it to the light, creating a single arc of your rainbow. In its positive phase fear can become your greatest ally as it cautions you to be wary and to avoid putting yourself and others in danger. However, once fear has completed its task, then thank it, let it go, and move on. In this way rather than being on habitual 'red alert' your sense of fear and danger will become more reliable as you will begin to trust it as a friend when it rises occasionally within you. When fear is ever-present, it becomes untrustworthy, telling you that everything, everyone, and life itself is scary, giving nowhere to turn to and no means of rising up and away from its grip.

If it is emotion that unites us, then it is mastery of our own emotional spheres that will free us and give us each more autonomy and more compassion. To become a master of your own self can strengthen a person enough to be of great service. To gain mastery is to hold all emotions in an expanded awareness, being able to access any of them at will, and being also willing to move through them and beyond into a place of stillness and calm. Think of a peaceful lake that is briefly disturbed by gusts or storms but can regain its state of serenity once the winds have passed. A true and profound gift of the water element is the ability to sink ever more deeply into the unknown, including the unknown territory of powerful emotions, but not to stay there, to keep moving, as to stay for too long is to risk becoming 'frozen' or 'stagnant'.

Mastering the emotions is key to creating the powerful internal space in which a person can become strong and adaptable enough to accommodate higher frequencies of energy without detriment to the health. Mental health is under the auspices of water and can be strengthened and safeguarded by training the mind to become still and tranquil through meditation and contemplation. This is a wonderful way of giving the mind a well-earned rest. By teaching the mind to rest it will repay you with renewed clarity. Muddled thinking can cause distortions and generate a dull and exhausted mind and body.

Sitting Gently with Your Mind

Choose a quiet place to sit.
Settle your body into an upright and balanced position where you feel supported and comfortable.
As your body settles, so will your mind.
Relax your face and relax your head and jaw.
As you listen to the sounds of life around you, allow your thoughts to start slipping away from your mind.
Imagine a fragment of light inside your head growing into a ball of beautiful white or golden light
The light fills the space within and around you, all unwanted thoughts slipping into it and being taken away.
It feels so clear and so restful in this light. Your entire body softens and flows with its radiance.
When you feel ready, start to draw the light back towards your head until it becomes a tiny spark again.
imagine the spark gently disappearing, leaving your mind and nervous system refreshed and well rested.

Rising Higher

Into the Realms of Gentleness and Wisdom

Water resonates with the deepest powers within; the ability to see and reflect upon the past and to change what is need in order to surge into the future. Consider for a moment the changing nature of water. It can shapeshift into many manifestations, from gentle autumn mists to drops of dew on a fresh spring morning. From a bubbling mountain brook to a mighty crashing waterfall. From the drip, drip of a leaking tap to a surging winter river. From a still and silent lake to the power of the ocean, a torrential summer rain storm to a stagnant garden pond. Water shows its changing face through all seasons and in all areas of nature. In a sense, water exerts control over the surroundings. Imagine the devastating effects of a river bursting its banks and flooding the surrounding area? The terrible effects of drought upon the land, crops and people? Rocks and cliffs eroded by the constant crashing waves? Water has a power and force of its own.

So too in people. The bladder meridian of the Water element surges up the forehead, over the top of the head and down either side of the spine, indicating its direct influence upon the brain and nervous system. Current understanding suggests that although we have thousands of thoughts in a single day, for the most part they are habitual and to an extent 'automatic'. We don't very often think new thoughts, and like the course of an ancient river, old thoughts have deeply forged their pathways in the brain and will stay that way until new courses or connections are made. These major internal rivers and tributaries in the brain and body have been forged by thoughts and events that have already happened in the course of life.

Memories and events from the past evoke emotional responses in the body stimulated by signals from the brain. Most people relive and re-experience past events, in particular traumatic ones, forging deep chasms of memory and emotion which can be relived every time these experiences are revisited through thought. Each re-living deepens the pathways. The sad thing is that although for most people, life creates happy events, happy memories and the emotions that accompany them, it is the traumas and difficulties that stay 'locked' into the memory and which stop us in our tracks for fear of them happening again. The other sad thing to remember is that each time they are remembered they happen again in the brain and body, and the emotional response is as 'real' as if they were happening in the present and not the past.

It is in this way that the present becomes a continuum of the past, and so on into the future. From this perspective, it seems unlikely that the future can be anything but a dull repetition of the past memories and past emotions. And of course, this trap is overseen by our Fear Demon who loves to imprison us through past mistakes and regret. Fear saps the will to even try to make life different. Sadly, thoughts become locked down into automatic pilot, well-guarded by our friend Fear Demon. He hates change, and will try any tricks to prevent the unknown, the new and as yet unrealised from emerging, as they are well outside his domain. The big trouble is that until thoughts change, beliefs and actions, emotions and activities are very unlikely to move, shift or create new riverways in your life.

The only way out of this prison is to change your mind! It's a refreshingly simple idea. It sounds easy, but like all habits, the habit of thoughts can take strength, power and will to break. To gain mastery over your own mind is to gain control over what enters your mind as thoughts, thereby gaining mastery over the messages that are released into your body as signals and emotion.

Begin the task of cleansing your mind. Wash away dark and difficult thoughts and memories from your nervous system. Think of this as a process of purification and imagine currents of fresh and clear water purifying the old, the outworn and the stagnant from your brain. Resolve to say a resounding 'No' to your mind as it tries to drag you into the dead and stagnant backwaters of fear, resentment, hurt and bitterness of the past. This will take all your power of will as the mind is persistent in its efforts to keep the old pathways alive by provoking the old memories. Like a worn-out record, they play on and on. It's sapping and exhausting for your reserves of energy, leaving little power left to bring about something new.

To create something fresh and new, fresh and new thoughts are needed. Bring new life to your present moments and to your unrealised future by letting outworn thoughts and energy become still and fade away, and to gradually become replaced by fresh and vibrant new currents of healthy qi. The future becomes bright, clear and ready to be stepped into.

As old thoughts arise,
feel the emotions that come with them.
Ask yourself whether you truly wish to keep all this alive within yourself?
Does it serve you, your loved ones, your future path?
Say these words as often as you need to
'I release all unwanted thoughts and memories from my past, and by doing so,
release myself from a prison of my own making.
I free my freewill.'

The bladder meridian speaks of the power of the future, of the unknown and of the wisdom needed to fulfil the callings of your soul. The big and challenging question is where to place your energy, attention and life force. Is your free will being compromised by the undercurrents of the past, or are you free to swim the tides of the unexplored future? Listen intently to the deep calling of your soul. Many people are filled with trepidation about facing the unknown, and up comes our old friend the Fear Demon, telling us how much 'safer' it is to stay within the confines of the familiar. Life, work, relationships could be dull, stagnant or unfulfilling, but still the Fear Demon whispers, "Stay with the known, stay safe."

Many people have secret wishes or desires for life to be somehow different. Perhaps there's a dream you have held most dear but with the passing of time lies dormant, stagnant and unrealised within. Perhaps you long to travel, to become successful, to learn something new? There are many things to experience in this wonderful world and many opportunities, if only you could shake off the fear. A magical way to help your new thoughts to thrive and your potential to become real is to superpower them with supercharged emotions such as joy or enthusiasm, which act as deep cleansers of unwanted fear.

Awakening into Higher Consciousness

The Wisdom Light of the Soul

With a joyful, peaceful and tranquil mind, comes the ability to reflect deeply, widely and fully enough to know the truth of your own life, and through this mirror to develop the insights to know yourself in a broader, deeper and higher sense. 'Who am I as a soul?' is a question of water, and one that can take much time to answer. When the disturbed waters of illusion, misperception, denial and avoidance clear, and the mud of excessive emotion settles to the bottom, the soul is reflected and revealed with a crystal clarity. Your soul deeply knows your own pathway and knows what experiences you need. It will prompt you to open up a potential that is right for you.

Implicit in experience and development is movement. The ability to move through and beyond life's difficulties and challenges is a highly powerful state of being. Nothing is denied or avoided but is faced with the will of accepting what cannot be changed and moving what can be changed. It is impossible to protect yourself from experiencing difficulties if it is in the interest of your own development to do so, and it can be the deepest traumas that bring about the highest awakenings. The personal will steps to centre stage to bring about the impetus to change and grow. The will says, "I am in charge of my own self." Pain and trauma split us wide open so that 'something else', perhaps the deeper and as yet unknown self, the light of soul, can come through. The truth is that we have the choice to shrink into the deeper recesses or to grow and come forwards through the experiences that life present, but the way of the will is to grow.

When the Water Comes Together

As the tributaries of beliefs, ideas, movements and changes come together into the great confluence of the river of your own life, you see all of life reflected around you. Your developing wisdom mirrors the truth that nothing is really separate, and all is one. All comes together in the great flow of life. As you believe in angels, so you can also believe in demons. As you carry light, you also carry darkness. Holding this awareness creates a bridge between these opposite polarities, enabling the awakening soul to carry an awareness of both the light and the dark. It flows between them both knowing that one cannot exist without balancing force of the other.

These reflections of truth arise from the deep waters – the essence and mystery of life. People who are blessed with a strong zhi are the mystics and the spiritual healers, the questers after the mysteries of hidden knowledge. The zhi are the guardians of the secret and the hidden. It is only after purifying the internal waters and cleansing deep karma that the highest and most sacred becomes available. Prayer, contemplation and meditation are all ways of purifying and calming the internal waters, and of steadying the everyday self, sufficiently to allow a flow of light into the unknown, the unrealised and the mysterious path of the soul.

Dark Night of the Soul

The Dark Night of the Soul is a phase where the hidden depths of being are encountered on the way to seeking 'something deeper'. Although dark depression and despair are awakened from the sleep of dormancy, the workings of the soul are at play. This is a difficult but vital phase of the healing journey and is a call to overcome internal shadows and, as portrayed in many mythologies, slay the demons of darkness. Your deep and hidden side has been with you on your journey, teaching you much about yourself, and by acknowledging and bringing this to the light of your conscious mind, fear begins to loosen its hold, evaporating into the higher spheres of wisdom.

This is a deeply personal state of being, and could be thought of as an initiation, so profound is its potential. It has the flavour of 'turning to face yourself' or, in Eastern philosophical terms, facing your karma. At this phase of the journey, you are alone and reflecting deeply upon who you are, on the meaning of life both on a personal level, and on the roles you have played in the lives of others. As a time of profound reflection, this phase can be tinged with regrets and with the horrors of hurt and wounds that have been cast upon your waters. There is often a deep awareness of the passage of time and of what may need to be healed, forgiven or purified before you embark on your next phase. There is a deepening awareness of mortality and of wanting to hold on to what was, and what has now been washed away in the rivers and tides of time.

My own experience of this phase lasted around two to three years, and looking back, I see it as time when I at last came face to face with myself. I spent much time alone and much time walking in nature as I wrestled with my internal demons and understood how they had played out in my own life. This was a point where I knew that I could sink into the mud and shadows as I had almost isolated myself apart from my work, which kept me functioning in the world while I sorted out my internal life. As I reflected on myself, I made some strong and conscious choices.

Through the darkness of deep despair, my will was at work, urging me to choose wisely. I spent much time in prayer and contemplation. I spent much time walking through rain and muddy fields internally prostrating myself at the feet of God and begging for forgiveness as a means of understanding, facing and healing those aspects of myself and my character that I no longer wished to take forward into my new phase. Over time, gently and carefully, I became purified of old and outworn habits, patterns, thoughts, beliefs and attitudes, and I became different. I felt in a strange way, as though I had awakened into a different 'me'. I know I looked different, and certainly didn't feel the same anymore. My whole being was undergoing a profound change as the forces of my soul came into play.

I began to feel lighter and gentler – to feel that at last I was flowing in harmony with life, rather than misusing my will and pitting myself against it. Obstacles no longer held too much sway with me, and life began to reposition itself more harmoniously within and around me. I felt then, and do now, as though I was well able to face myself, as all my previously hidden fears and doubts no longer held me captive. I became under the auspices of a higher will, with which I now align myself.

Well Meditation

Imagine a well.

It is strongly built and sinks deeply into the recesses of the ground.
There is water at the bottom of the well. Fresh, clean and clear on the surface,
but it's depths are hidden.
You are like this well.
Your experiences, losses and gains have built the strong walls and have sunk
the well to unimaginable depths.
All you are, and all you have been through and are going through adds more
bricks to the walls and more depth.
Gentle water falls as rain, mingling with underground springs to create the new
waters of life and experiences yet to come, fresh and untasted.
These waters come together with the wisdom gained from experience
producing deep sustenance of soul on which to draw.

Becoming Wisdom

Trauma and loss can tear deep caverns way down inside us. It takes an attitude of profound inner gentleness for the fresh waters of new beginnings to soothe these wounds. When this happens, you will emerge as a deep and gentle well of experience and wisdom for self and others. The well is powerful, strong and able to replenish itself from the rich and profound waters of life and inner divine light. From this well comes the deeper language of soul, and questions such as 'For what was I born?' can be reflected upon, informing your life with new depths and the riches and power of purpose.

Fear seeks to hold on tightly, while the wisdom of the soul speaks of allowing it all to flow gently softening the way with love and grace, allowing new phases of life to emerge, beautiful, powerful and wise. The deep reflective mirrors of water show that nothing is truly lost. All that you have been has created who you have become, as a huge reflection of your journey. There is no loss, only learning and experience the wisdom gained through these to flow onwards.

A Blessing of Water

May your life
Be blessed with light power and gentle streams of love,
And both the ancient and the new be etched upon your face.
May you reach for all that you are.
And may your rivers forge pathways of beauty upon this earth,
As you swim the higher waves of grace
and answer the tides of your calling.
May you be forever uplifted by the song of the divine within your soul,
Riding the crest of your wave.

Chapter 7

Reflections

In this book, we have now encountered and become familiar with each of the five elements in its own sphere or phase of qi. However, a profound teaching of the five elements is of relationship and community. Each element, as we have seen, has a 'task' and a role, but it is the coming together of all these tasks and roles that completes the whole picture or the whole person, or the whole cycle of nature.

The elements all exist both individually and in relationship, having particular and vital connections with all the others, and in their coming together, they create something whole and complete. The highest aspiration for any of us is to encompass all of the resonances and teachings of all elements equally and appropriately, and not become 'stuck' in a box, or 'stuck' in just one season or stance towards life. Just as nature cannot ever be 'always springtime', or 'always summer' etc., so we too need to learn how to encompass the varied flows of life.

Try becoming open to the elements that are not your natural environment and recognise and appreciate how they each reveal themselves in you.

The Water within You

If water is not your environment, can you still yourself enough to become reflective and to gain wisdom from the teachings and teachers in your life?

Can you sink deeply and quietly within?

Can you stop fighting the currents and 'go with the flow' when life carries you on its tides?

The Wood within You

If you are not a 'woody' individual, can you envision and create from your imagination?

Can you make your dreams come true and become author of your own life?

Do you have goals and aspirations that assert your own growth?

Are you growing to fulfil your own blueprint?

The Fire within You

If you are not naturally a fire spirit, how does fire reveal itself as the height of creative expression in you?

How are your social interactions and relationships?

Can you love fully and openly?

How is your joy, your laughter and spontaneity?

The Earth within You

If earth is not where you stand, what do you manifest and how fully can you encompass and emanate feelings of gratitude and compassion?

Can you stand up for what matters to you and do you have the capacity to walk your own path?

Can you care enough about the plight of someone else to walk for a while in their shoes?

The Metal within You

If metal is not your natural element, do you know the depth of the treasures of your own soul?

Can you let go of what might be holding you back from moving to the next phase of your life, and find the inspiration to move forward?

Do you have the courage to enter the profound silence?

Each of the elements teaches of an aspect of being human, and to encompass all of them is to encourage expansion beyond the familiar and into the unknown and as yet unrevealed spheres of yourself. Learning to make good use of the seasonal flows and changes allows each of them to tell their own story through the stories of the natural world. As you become a keen observer of the changes in nature, you will come to experience these phases being reflected in yourself as living energies and the spirit of ever-changing life. This the natural law of which, as beings of earth, we are a part.

Different ages and phases of your life are also governed by their own element.

Water

Water holds the polarities of opposites, encompassing both the quiet and the powerful, and holding the potential of life. Water oversees all stages of the developmental processes from the initial growth in the watery world of the womb, to birth to the changes from child to adult, to death and beyond.

Wood

Wood is the rising lightforce of qi, initiating the vital zest of youthful exuberance. As the spirit of creativity, this rising energy urges the dreaming and growth needed to find out about who you are as an individual, and where you fit as an into this puzzle of life. What are you here to create, to offer, to contribute?

Fire

Fire is the furthest expansion and rising of qi and brings into being your expansive maturity. This is when you reach your peak, develop confidence and revel in living life to the full as a mature adult.

Earth

Late summer is the phase of life when energy become more stable, neither rising, nor beginning to fall away, and offers time to take stock and evaluate your life so far, and to understand what matters to you.

Metal

With autumn begins the falling away of natural energies and might encompass a sense of grief for more youthful times. It is potentially the time of midlife crisis when you begin to feel the passage of time. With this sense of the limits of your own life span may come an urgency to do or achieve the things that can no longer be put off. This is the point at which you may discover how to let go of what is no longer appropriate and encompass and place value on, what is more relevant.

Return to Water

Then begins the sinking where qi descends to its deepest level and brings in the winter years of wisdom and old age – the reflective times of a life well lived, and into the cycle of death and beyond.

In this way, the elements can take on different meanings and are not restricted to changes in a yearly cycle, but also teach of the cycles of a developing and maturing life. From understanding where you sit elementally, you can begin to expand and grow towards opening to all the others. You may understand that you have a second element that sits comfortably within your outlook and preferences, and beyond that one, towards a third, and so on.

As your awareness opens to a more expanded perception, it becomes easier to move beyond your own filters, becoming more open and receptive to fluctuations in the natural forces of the life of which we are all a part. Summer could not exist if not for winter laying the foundations and the potential for growth. Winter could not exist without the heat of fire igniting the spirit of life. Spring could not come bursting into life without the decomposing forces of autumn to produce rich soil. Life could not survive without water and would have nowhere to place itself without earth. As each element comes into its own phase and qi rises and falls, movement is created, and it is this powerful and harmonious movement that sustains the life that we know and experience.

By gaining more familiarity with the essence of the elements, their deeper teachings become revealed. Water and fire as overseeing elements of winter and summer are the elements of the two extremes of the year and hold a strong axis around which the other elements can position themselves. For the purposes of this level of understanding, water and fire can be considered as the primary elements, being opposite in polarity, the yin of winter and the yang of summer. On the other side of the axis are placed the wood of spring and the metal of autumn. These two elements also hold each other in a strong relationship as they too can be considered opposites. Wood is the element of the creative spirit which brings about the force of birth and new life, while metal holds the sword of death, cutting through everything that needs to fall away. These two influences move around the axis of fire and water, needing just the right conditions of heat and cold, light and dark, expansion and contraction, to fulfil their tasks.

The fifth element of earth holds a different purpose, which is perhaps more complex in nature. Earth has a unique role – that of holding all life on this planet in materialised form. It is the essential force that not only has its own season of late summer, acting as a level phase between the rising of growth and the falling of decay, it is also the holding force, or bridge, between all the elements. Earth facilitates the passage of one element or season into the next, and so on, to create a whole year or a whole movement of a life.

You may have noticed some subtle 'golden' days towards the end of one season and the beginning of another, where both seasons come and go for a while between the old one that is being moved through and beyond, and the new one that is emerging. This is the connecting force created by the power of earth. Earth, quite simply, holds the whole show together, exerting a gravitational pull which controls everything in relation to everything else, holding the environment and the right conditions through which natural forces are able to rise and fall in a creative and life-giving cycle.

As we have already seen, the elements have essential tasks within the body, mind and spirit, and together form a deep sense of movement and community within an individual. Each organ or process has a very specific and vital role and task to undertake, but without all the other organs and processes working harmoniously, the individual ones become meaningless as the whole system soon breaks down. Each aspect, or element, as we know, has its own energetic movement and overseeing spirit, its particular emotional depth and its rising awareness, all coming together to act as mirrors into the incredible complexity that is life. Each phase then, however seemingly tiny or insignificant, has a task and a vital part to play.

So it is with you. You may feel at times when life is difficult, that who you are or what you do is not significant or important, but perhaps you can now begin to see that you are very important and play an essential role in the emergence of life as a whole. You play a vital role in the intricate dance of life. Dancing implies harmonious movement, and it is this flowing movement that is not only necessary for the creation and facilitation of good health, but also makes life more colourful and interesting. How drab to stay locked into one phase that keeps repeating itself. Times of pausing to take stock of what's happening in and around you are very much part of a healthy life, but it's the change, and the movements and tidal waves that are created by change that add complexity and texture.

However, too much movement becomes an imbalance, as does too little. Here we are reminded of the teachings of yin and yang – movement and stillness and the harmony of encompassing opposites, such as light and dark, cool and heat, night and day. Internal movements of harmonious flowing qi manifest a creative and fulfilling life, coupled with the pauses and stillness of quieter and deeper reflective times. It's a habitual lack of movement that we all need to be wary of when life seems to grind to a halt, and we hit brick wall after brick wall of nothing happening because nothing can change or shift. At these times, we need to consider what life is trying to mirror and what can be perceived, learnt or understood from this reflection.

Begin to extend your perception to look at the possibility of your own internal landscape as a reflection of what's happening in the world of nature. When you are next feeling melancholic, down, tearful, or stuck, look outwards at what's happening around you. Look at how other people are feeling too. Is there something that you are experiencing that is also shared by others? If this is the case, then it may be because you are all responding to a phase of qi. There may have been a swift change in temperature, or the movement from one season to another may have been too rapid for you to integrate and adapt to the changes. Maybe the weather has been 'stuck' for an overly long period, too hot, too dry or too wet and grey. You are potentially mirroring what is happening in nature, as an opportunity to look again at the movements of life within yourself.

Here is an example of what I mean. From my own perspective, the change from an unusually hot and prolonged summer to a sudden drop in temperature and the onset of the change towards autumn was swift this year, with natural qi falling rapidly away, and little felt of the stabilising energetic of the earth element of late summer (Note, late summer comes between summer and autumn). This change and instability in what was taking place in nature was mirrored within both myself, some friends and some of my patients. Many of us were feeling as though we had suddenly lost our footing, or suddenly feeling depressed or melancholic, seemingly 'out of the blue'. If this was a shared experience, then this meant that it was both personal and impersonal.

The phase of late summer with its gentle but stabilising energy of mother earth was overly short this year, resulting in many people feeling sad, bereft and insecure. Where was our harvest time? Where was the nurturing and nourishing mother energy, that feeds and sustains us before the descent towards autumn and winter?

The texture of energy of late summer, as has already been discovered earlier in this book, is the qi of holding and compassion. This vital phase this year seemed short and over too soon for many people to have sufficient time to make the necessary internal adjustments.

The earth element, whose primary time arises as late summer, is about stabilising and assimilating as a respite from the high fires of summer and before the descent into the loss of autumn. The lack of this stabilising energetic was mirrored in the difficulties that people were experiencing. There was a definite theme to people's struggles this year, and it was the theme of friendships and relationships. With the sudden drop in energy came the need to know and to feel the sustaining nature of close relationships, and many people began to question these, asking who their true friends really were, and the meaning and nature of true friendship? I too experienced the loss of a very close friendship with someone that I had played the role of 'mother' to. The loss was sudden and abrupt, like the change in temperature and energetics.

This phase of energy proved to be one of testing the personal matrix of relationships as emotional anchors, revealing the need to look at how the earth element resonates within your domain. How secure do you feel within yourself, regardless of external shifts and drifts? Can you nurture yourself when the need arises? How we experience these movements in qi are indicative of how steady, or otherwise, we are within our own energetic domain, and can be a wake-up call to have another peek within to understand what is being revealed. 'What does this tell me about myself?' is a very potent question to ask of yourself whenever you are face to face with either an unfamiliar or a regular and familiar set of emotional responses or if you are feeling sudden changes which seem to mirror nature.

As nature lives in me, so I live in nature.

When your mood changes, or you feel 'stuck' in an emotional state, practice opening your perception outwards towards nature for some answers. Perhaps the seasons are 'out of sync', with one season being unrelentingly long, or the seasons may be changing rapidly with resultant ups and downs which undermine your natural sense of equilibrium. Overly long and grey spells may well become mirrored within you. How does this greyness reveal itself and what does this show you about the workings of the elements of metal and water within you? Some people may love those times as opportunities for quiet, for study and for reflection, while others may feel lonely and despondent. There are no rights or wrongs, but just questions to be revealed and perhaps answered through your growing levels of awareness. Learn to look both outwards towards nature and inwards towards yourself, balancing internal with external and yin with yang for your information and your answers to guide you into your deepening awareness.

I am of Spirit, I am of Earth.
I am of the moon and stars, the sun and the turnings of time.
I walk with grace, with open loving heart.
I am of the rushing rivers, the contours of hill and valley.
I am of the spiking shoot, the clap of thunder,
The souls longing to be.
I am of Spirit, I am of Earth.

Chapter 8

The Path of the Heart as a High Trajectory of Healing and Living

Heart light

There is a phrase –
'Getting to the heart of something'.
Some deeper place within us knows that the heart changes everything.
Just as sunlight reveals colour and brightness, changing the landscape in an instant,
So the heart has equal capacity,
Rapidly transforming everything with its
touch of light.

When life and all its movements of experience and feeling are lived through the raised level of an awakened and loving heart, then what previously appeared drab, dull, depressed and dreary, now ignites, brightens, lifts and magically transforms. Like sunlight emerging from behind the clouds changes the landscape, so your loving radiance can influence everything around and within you. You have all that you need: your own instant, transforming beautiful heart light deeply within you.

The heart offers a doorway to the soul, and when you are under the direction of your soul, then you are free from previous limitations, which fall away as the mists and shadows that were previously veiling the directing power of your internal sunlight. You are now following your highest trajectory that you as a human can follow. From this perspective, life changes and lightens. You may discover that what previously seemed important, no longer holds sway. The cravings of the overly stimulated and tired mind are free to flutter away like butterflies in the breeze, and more important things may come to the fore and request your attention.

The section on the Spirits of Fire earlier in this book described the sacred nature of the heart, which in traditional Chinese Medicine has a very special place, being the sovereign and honoured as being central to the overall health and wellbeing of a person, from the highest spheres of the spirit, through the mental, emotional and physical spheres. It is possible, of course, to function perfectly adequately in life with a closed and barren heart, but life tends to mirror that back, revealing itself as closed and barren, joyless and lacking.

Pure and Clear Space of the Loving Heart

Meditation to Help in the Practice of Radiating Your Own Heart Light.

Imagine your heart as a pure and clear space.
Take your attention towards the centre of your chest, allowing your thoughts to rest here.
Within the centre of this space, imagine a tiny and pulsating hub of light, emanating pure and clear colours, weaving and spiralling to infuse the whole of your heart space.
Such exquisite beauty.
Now imagine this light leaving your heart in a stream of colour and travelling out into life, gently encompassing the world in its radiance. Here it connects with other heart lights and creates a living light network for all to tap into. Take your time to experience the feelings created by making these connections.
Hold the energy of this network for a few moments
Gently return your heart light to yourself, encouraging it to flow through and around any areas of yourself or your life that are in need of the presence of healing light. When you are ready,
gently and lovingly centre yourself back into your
Pure and Clear Heart Space.

Now is the time for the awakening of the heart. We are living in the age of the emerging heart and soul, gradually transitioning away from the hard and factual reality of the industrialised era, towards a more far reaching, broader perspective, where in this age of technology, anything is possible. The journey can be turbulent as reality continues to make its shifts. Quantum science now tells us that nothing is fixed, and that everything is subject to changes from any number of influences, meaning that everything exists in relation to something else. Now we know for sure that how you are affects how I am, and how I react affects how you react.

This is great news for the mystics and healers and those of us who already believed this to be true, as it creates a more credible platform for our beliefs, and this softer and more fluid approach now makes possible, what was previously deemed impossible. It is this belief that enables me, and many others, to help people with whom factual reality, and in some instances, the medical profession has reached the end of the road, as some levels of illness confound the rational approach and people are now increasingly awakening to take responsibility for their own health and wellbeing, asking the deeper questions – 'Do I create my own health and therefore ill health? Is there more I can do in this area of my life?' This book has gone someway to answering these and many more questions, offering profound tools for breaking old ties and old ways. We are no longer isolated, and we all matter both as individuals and as connecting points for the whole movement of life. The calling is to be strong and gentle, open aware, wise and ready to move, adapt and transform old and worn ties and ways of approaching life.

The scientific approach has revealed so many fascinating and detailed facts and has hugely broadened the scope of knowledge, making life-changing advances in its areas of expertise. Technology makes possible what was previously only a dream. Information is available effortlessly at the press of a button, and we can link up with anyone in ant part of the world at any time. The world is unrecognisable as the same world of fifty or a hundred years ago. However, it's vitally important that each of us retains who we are, and that we don't get too lost in technology as being the answer to everything. Through loving hearts and the path of the awakening soul, we can begin to make significant differences to our own lives, to the lives of those we love and to the vast field of grace that surrounds and encompasses all people. By using the knowledge that we are interconnected gives us the power to make vast and positive changes. We live in an era where scientific thought and discovery dovetail exquisitely with mystical and spiritual thought, and here lies the truth. What was once divided now reflects the truth of the other, giving new life to the mystical law 'All is One'.

It's interesting to note that although ancient Chinese masters gave the status of sovereign to the heart, they did not recognise the brain as having any particular or major significance over the other processes, viewing it as an integral part of the workings of the nervous system, yet we in our Western way of thinking, have to a greater or lesser extent, pushed it to the forefront becoming enslaved to its way. There is a worldwide movement towards becoming 'mindful', as a very useful way of taming the mind and changing and reprogramming habitual or destructive thoughts and behaviour. Through this practice, many of us have learnt much about the workings of our own minds, enabling those of us who are willing, to gain an awareness about this mysterious world and its ways.

Fire and Water

The way of the mind becomes different when infused by the radiance of the heart, and when they are connected and move as one, (here's that theme again), life begins to flow on a new trajectory. We have been given both a mind and a heart, so why not see what happens when the two are integrated and learn to work harmoniously and in relationship with each other? Life appears very different when viewed from the heart, and now is just the perfect time to 'change our minds' (water) and open our hearts (fire) and bring the two aspects of self together.

Fire and water are opposite in nature but hold each other in a strong relationship. In terms of the teaching of the five elements, water holds dominion over winter, and fire over summer. Something interesting happens when two opposites come together, and the ancients called this magical process Alchemy.

Water and fire have a controlling influence over each other, creating a point of balance. Fire warms water causing movement and change, while water regulates the damaging effects of fire by dousing excessive flames or ravaging heat. Fire without water creates drought in the landscape, and water without fire creates flooding.

Something truly magical happens when fire and water come together, and there are many times in the natural world where this can be observed in the course of a day. As I sit writing, I am lucky enough to witness the sun coming and going between the clouds and now and again casting dazzling displays of diamonds across the lake. It's quite simply an incredible sight, made even more beautiful by the contrast of the grey clouds and the reflection of that greyness into the lake when the sun disappears. Consider too, how sunlight looks shining upon a rolling ocean. Dazzling light upon the crashing waves creates a dynamism of flashing dancing rainbows.

When fire and water truly come together, they create more than each on their own. They seem to create something extra, that can't really be named, but that you and I can feel and experience as something beautiful, uplifting, powerful and enriching. If the water element holds the mind and the fire element holds the heart, then, as in the examples of where fire and water meet in nature, we can see what may happen when heart and mind come together. Suddenly the potential for 'something else', which cannot truly be named, but only experienced as beautiful, uplifting, powerful and enriching becomes possible. In my terms, this is the light of soul, in your terms it may be the realm of the Higher self, God or Goddess. All are here and all are possible in this domain.

Fire and Water

Go in your imagination to a tranquil lake.
Imagine that it is early in the day and the sun has yet to rise.
All is quiet and still, with night ending and day yet to emerge.
Gradually as though coming to birth, the sun peeps above the horizon, casting shafts of new light across the gentle water.
Higher and higher, it soars and with the majesty of a god, holds its place in the sky.
All is glowing and radiant around you, all has become infused with life.
Colours dance within the light, bouncing off the rippling contours of the lake.

So it is with you, as the love and radiance from your heart ignites the depths and beauty of your soul.
You are the sun and the lake, fire and water, love and wisdom.
Profound, beautiful, eternal.

As the heart begins to open and to hold sway, its radiance awakens a deeper and more hidden side within. In some traditions, this loving vibration is heralded as the energy of the feminine nature, but whatever its nature, its radiance can lift, transform ignite and bring together what was previously separated. This is just the resonance needed to awaken the hidden side of life (the shadowlands), that to a greater or lesser degree, has been waiting in the wings, or at the bottom of our internal lakes, waiting to be awakened and acknowledged. How can any of us fully express ourselves, or discover why we're here if part of us lives in hiding? As women become more present in everyday life and the strive is towards the balance of masculine and feminine in the outside world, so the calling is to balance them within, each being a mirror of the other. As men, the call has been to spend more time within the family and to encompass a more emotionally connected and caring side, an aspect of being that was previously the domain of women in our culture.

This uniting of polarities creates an energetic of equilibrium, which acts as a very stable matrix for the incoming soul but can also produce chaos as huge changes take place within the individual and the societies in which we are living and expressing these changes. We need day and night, light and dark, heat and cold to create a whole, and so it is with each of us, whether man or woman, the call is to integrate and balance masculine and feminine, the heart and the mind, the rational self and the loving self, and to bring it all out of hiding.

Taking Thinking into the Heart: Here is a very simple idea to try for yourself. Next time, you are face with a crisis in your life or something that is challenging or 'problematic'. Perhaps you feel hurt or upset by the words, actions or circumstances of someone you care about, or you might be faced with something that to your thoughts seems insurmountable and you just do not know which way to turn. You may feel in the grip of this 'something', which takes such a tight hold of you that you can concentrate on little else. Your thoughts spin endlessly around in your mind, holding tightly on to you and allowing little space for anything else.

When this happens, just allow your mind free reign for a few moments, let it wrestle with the 'monster' of your hurt, worry, or upset, and let yourself become consumed by the reactions, responses and emotions that engulf you. Allow yourself a little time to fully experience this level of your reality. In my own case, it proved almost too much to cope with, such was the power of my emotional anguish and mental turmoil. I felt tired, nauseous and withdrawn. My mind was lurching between the extremes of revenge and an apathetic and sentimental form of forgiveness, and I just had no idea how I was going to find way through this torment.

After experiencing all that you need to experience for a few moments, change your focus by drawing your attention to the centre of your chest and the region of your heart. You may need an act of will to achieve this and to stop yourself from returning to your mind games. You may need to place your hands across your heart or draw them together as though in prayer as a physical signal for your awareness to follow. Breathe steadily and focus your attention. When you are safely within the realm of your heart, allow the same problem, challenge or hurt to unfold once more, and wait for your reactions. Keep your awareness and your breathing steady and focussed.

I'm almost certain that your perspective, responses and emotions will be now be quite different. You will almost certainly find a way through your crisis that hadn't before been apparent, and you will feel in control of it rather than being controlled. Within moments, you will feel very different. Your awareness may keep tugging back into your 'head thinking' but hold it in your heart as steadily as you can. From the perspective of the heart, your world can very quickly change. In my own case, I now felt that I could easily cope with the situation, which hadn't changed at all in the outside world, but was completely transformed in my interior world. Quite unexpectedly and suddenly, I was no longer a victim! The change was miraculous, and I and was able to practice forgiveness from the very healing and transformative depths of my heart, because this was where my challenge lay. You may be different, but this illustration is intended to indicate the speed at which something can be transformed by bringing the heart and mind together. You can quite literally, move the mountains of your burdens! I remember laughing with incredulity at the joyful simplicity of my new discovery, playing with it as if I'd found a new toy. How easy to change my life!

This simple but crucial discovery, made some years ago, did change everything. I began to consciously centre myself in my heart as my new way and my new approach, and everything began to transform. I felt so and awake and moved to a different rhythm. One that was softer, easier, lighter. I noticed that my mind became more useful as it was now freed from the things that it was largely unable to deal with. This is where I choose to remain, away from the fixed domain of the mind but connected with its clear-thinking processes, as this is its undeniable strength.

Take care of your emotions by offering them to the realms of your heart and allowing love to transform them into higher feelings and a higher intention, one that your mind alone cannot conceive of. The mind is then free to deliver information and rational thinking, which is its true domain. To free the mind from the arena of the emotions is a very good thing, as the mind doesn't handle them too well and together they can create havoc. The mind is then cleared of what it can't handle, allowing it to become open and flowing and free to awaken to higher realities, thoughts and knowledge. Love changes the world, and I had made this discovery in such a simple, but profound, way. It is often when we are at our most desperate that we need to make the changes that perhaps we have previously known about but haven't had the time, energy or capacity to bother with. I recommend that you bother with this one.

The Sovereign

We now understand that Chinese medicine bequeaths much reverence upon the heart. It is viewed as the most profound and sacred part of a person. Being so revered, it is honoured as the gracious Sovereign over all the elements and their tasks and workings, meaning that all processes of the body mind and spirit have a level of responsibility towards the heart. The heart needs to be protected by sacred space so that the highest flows of love can be generated and emerge unimpeded into your life. This love is a grace and is selfless, pure and of the spirit. In a greater context, we see reflected the responsibility that we all have in life towards love as being central to healthy life.

My work as acupuncturist and soul healer has taught me the power of love as far from being sentimental, or in some way 'weak', is a very tangible and potent healing vibration. It is though love that a field of harmony in which all elements of a person can be explored and awakened to their most radiant potential is created. In this field of grace, all aspects of an individual, can emerge, now having the capacity to flourish, and to create potent and iridescent rivers of light where the soul emerges at its most luminous.

The denser and heavier energetics, which in this book I have described as being the shadow side, exert a restrictive force upon the opening of the heart and incoming soul. I have come to know, many times over, that it is through understanding, working with and ultimately encompassing these lower resonances, that a higher resonance can begin to take effect, easing the way for the higher trajectory of the heart and soul to exert their influence on your life. When this takes place, your life can change – mine most certainly did! My health and energy levels have certainly improved, and I have a very different stance in life. I have a renewed strength and rarely suffer from any symptoms or conditions. I used to be afflicted by swings in mood, general fearfulness and chronic anxiety. I had a chronically bad back and my thyroid levels were low. All these states have become like a distant dream, and my life has taken on a new trajectory. I have never felt this good! It is not to say that life has ceased its challenges, but perhaps I don't take everything so personally, as I am now better equipped to keep moving myself. I feel that this has made me more 'useful' to life and to people as I no longer feel so 'weighted'.

When the heart takes its rightful place as overseer and sovereign, then all the difficulties of the lower nature no longer have jurisdiction and over time simply fall by the wayside, as something that was previously useful, but is now no longer in alignment with higher-conscious living. These parts of yourself may still be present in the memory banks of learning and wisdom, and may prove very useful as an indication of where your focus is now and as a warning never to return to this way. Fear no longer holds centre stage in the palace of the heart, it has now been elevated to its rightful place as messenger of danger. The elements can flow naturally, acting as a light matrix for the soul, which fully enters into a person's life through the open and loving heart. Aspects of the personality which are inhibitive, restrictive, selfish or unkind are no longer relevant and no longer sustainable in the domain of the higher nature.

We could now say that the emotional nature has been transformed and no longer holds dominion. This is not to say we become unfeeling or unemotional, far from it, and are possibly more sensitive and awake to ours and other people's feelings. We now become masters of our emotions as we understand their processes and their messages and will not be dragged down into their destructive cycles. We know when to feel strong emotions, and when to let them pass through and away. The influence of the heart transforms the harmful aspects of the emotional forces into pure feeling. Next time, you are beset by an emotional storm, try the following.

Transforming Emotions through the Loving Heart

Take three deep breaths, in through the nose and powerfully exhaling through the mouth, like a strong sigh.

Give voice to your emotions.

For example, "I feel incredibly sad because…

I feel very angry because…

Allow yourself to feel as you do for a moment or two, noticing the effects on your body.

You may feel hot, cold. Your pulse may be racing, your palms clammy, or you may be weeping, or even frozen and locked down.

The noticing and acknowledgement of how you are, will create a little space between you and your emotional state, as you begin to become witness and observer of yourself.

Is your reaction appropriate to the conditions that have arisen?

Are you overreacting?

Do you habitually feel this way?

Would you rather feel a different way?

The more often you can act as your own observer, the more space you will create between you and your reactions. This space can be just what is needed for you to gain the awareness to make an empowered choice over how you are reacting.

This in itself is often sufficient to remove the charge and to abate the reactions. Even if this is the case, please do the following.

Draw attention to your heart by lightly tapping the centre of your sternum with your fingertips.

This will alert your mind to the idea that something else is happening.

Encourage your attention to stay with your tapping fingers, and when your awareness is reliably centred in your heart, then you either stop tapping and allow stillness to emerge.

Allow your focus to stay in the realm of the heart, making your way towards the loving and peaceful spot deep within the centre of your heart.

Here rest a while

The voice of your heart will give a new perspective to your emotional field. It will give you healing messages and will begin to transform these emotions into the higher and finer feelings of the heart.

When emotions run strongly and deeply, this can take a lot of focus to achieve, but please be kind to yourself as you practice, and be willing to heal your emotional reactions, transforming them into a powerful source of energy.

Emotions can be very draining and exhausting, and an emotional storm can leave you feeling depleted and washed out.

Over time, these very emotions will become a source of power, as your will have attained a level of mastery, not allowing them to ravage and destroy you."

Love creates a powerful field of grace. When the heart, mind and emotions come together into this higher field of love, huge amounts of positive energy is created, and when difficult and irksome emotions are transformed into higher feelings, and the mind joins into alignment too, a higher field of resonance is generated which can not only transform your life, but can have a potent effect on all other people who come into your sphere of influence, which can become wider than you realise.

Love is the way of light and the way of the
empowered healer.

Here I stand, with my feet upon the bountiful Earth,
and my heart reaching Heavenward
Empowered by love.
Radiant with Spirit
Flowing with Compassion
Giving
Receiving

I am nurtured
I am cherished
I am the light of my own Soul,
And I have journeyed far and wide,
Across the eternal seas of
Wisdom